FINRA SERIES 7

Practice Tests

TABLE OF CONTENTS

INTRODUCTION

ABOUT TRIVIUM TEST PREP

Trivium Test Prep uses industry professionals with decades' worth of knowledge in their fields, proven with degrees and honors in law, medicine, business, education, the military, and more, to produce high-quality test prep books for students.

Our study guides are specifically designed to increase any student's score, regardless of his or her current skill level. Our books are also shorter and more concise than typical study guides, so you can increase your score while significantly decreasing your study time.

WE WANT TO HEAR FROM YOU

Here at Trivium Test Prep our hope is that we not only taught you the relevant information needed to pass the exam, but that we helped you exceed all previous expectations. Our goal is to keep our guides concise, show you a few test tricks along the way, and ultimately help you succeed in your goals.

On that note, we are always interested in your feedback. To let us know if we've truly prepared you for the exam, please email us at feedback@triviumtestprep.com. Feel free to include your test score!

Your success is our success. Good luck on the exam and your future ventures.

Sincerely,

-Trivium Test Prep Team-

PRACTICE TEST #1

1. Use the following information for the question below:

Zee	ACME	FADSLD	DDE
10.00	7s30	10.000s40	4s15s

Which of the following statements are correct regarding Zee?

I.	1,000 shares traded
II.	100 shares traded
III.	100 shares traded at 10.00

A. I only

B. II only

C. III only

D. II and III

2. A customer, in a cash account, purchases 1 DEF 60 Put @ $2 and sells 1 DEF 70 Put @ $6 when the price of ABC stock is trading at $63. What is the maximum loss for this position?

A. $200

B. $400

C. $600

D. $800

3. Use the following information for the question below:

Zee	ACME	FADSLD	DDE
10.00	7s30	10.000s40	4s15s

Which of the following statements are correct regarding the trade in FAD?

I.	1,000 shares traded
II.	100 shares traded
III.	100 shares traded at 10.00

A. I and III

B. I and IV

C. II and III

D. II and IV

4. A customer purchases 1 XYZ 60 Call @ $5 and 1 XYZ 60 Put @ $3 when the price of XYZ is trading at $62. The maximum loss for this position is:

A. $0

B. $300

C. $500

D. $800

5. Which one of the following statements is correct?

    A. An American stock option can be exercised any time prior to expiration.

    B. The buyer of a call is obligated to purchase one hundred shares of the underlying security at the strike price.

    C. At expiration, a stock option becomes a market order.

    D. The seller of a put is bearish on the market.

6. A customer paid $200 to purchase a call on ABC stock with a strike price of $30. What does the market price of ABC stock have to be for the customer to break even on this option?

    A. $28

    B. $32

    C. $30

    D. $23

7. What is the fundamental value of a put with a strike price of $20 and a market price of $18?

    A. $0

    B. $200

    C. $2,000

    D. $2

8. A customer purchased a put with a strike price of 25 when the option was quoted at 1. What is the maximum profit the customer can earn on this investment?

    A. $2,500

    B. $24

    C. $2,499

    D. $2,400

9. Which of the following options are in-the-money?

    | I. | A call with a strike price of $30 with the underlying security priced at $32 |
    | II. | A call with a strike price of $30 with the underlying security priced at $29 |
    | III. | A put with a strike price of $30 with the underlying security priced at $32 |
    | IV. | A put with a strike price of $30 with the underlying security priced at $29 |

    A. I and IV

    B. I and III

    C. II and IV

    D. II and III

10. A customer wrote a 35 put on XYZ stock. The total option price was $125. The customer does not currently own any shares of XYZ stock. What is the customer's maximum loss on the option position?

    A. $3,375

    B. The losses are unlimited.

    C. $3,625

    D. $125

11. The writer of a naked call has a maximum profit that is ___ and a maximum loss that is ___.

    A. equal to the call premium; unlimited

    B. unlimited; equal to the strike price

    C. equal to the strike price plus the call premium; unlimited

    D. unlimited; equal to the call premium

12. What is the ex-dividend date for cash settlement trades?

    A. four business days before the record date

    B. five business days before the record date

    C. the same day as the record date

    D. one day after the record date

13. Which one of the following statements is correct concerning warrants?

   A.   Warrants generally provide voting rights.

   B.   A warrant is a short-term option on shares of stock.

   C.   Warrants do NOT pay dividends.

   D.   Warrants cover 100 shares of the underlying stock.

14. You can purchase options on which of the following?

I.	Interest rates
II.	Currencies
III.	ETFs
IV.	Indexes

   A.   I and III

   B.   III and IV

   C.   I, II, III, and IV

   D.   II, III and IV

15. A customer, in a cash account, purchases 1 ABC 50 Call @ $7 and sells 1 ABC 40 Call @ $4 when the price of ABC stock is trading at $45. What is the maximum loss for this position?

   A. $300

   B. $400

   C. $700

   D. $1,000

16. If there is no activity in a client's account, how often must the brokerage firm send a statement to the client?

   A.   monthly

   B.   quarterly

   C.   semi-annually

   D.   yearly

17. A customer, in a cash account, purchases 1 ABC 50 Call @ $7 and sells 1 ABC 40 Call @ $4 when the price of ABC stock is trading at $45. Which of the following best describes this position's strategy?

I.	Bearish
II.	Bullish
III.	Debit
IV.	Credit

   A.   I and III

   B.   II and III

   C.   II and IV

   D.   I and IV

18. Use the following information for the question below.

Zee	ACME	FADSLD	DDE
10.00	7s30	10.000s40	4s15s

   How many shares of ACME traded?

   A.   7

   B.   70

   C.   700

   D.   7,000

19. What is the ad valorem tax on a property with an assessed value of $550,000, a current market value of $535,000, and a tax rate of 16 mills?

   A. $8,800

   B. $9,600

   C. $10,400

   D. $12,800

20. Firm X is a member of a selling group, while Firm Y is not a participant in the offering. If Firm X sells a small number of shares to Firm Y at a price that is slightly below the public offering price, this would be considered:

   A.   illegal

   B.   reallowance

   C.   retention

   D.   undercutting

21. A customer purchases 1 XYZ 60 Call @ $5 and 1 XYZ 60 Put @ $3 when the price of XYZ is trading at $62. If the price of XYZ moves to $75 and the customer exercises the call, what is her profit/loss?

A. $700 profit

B. $700 loss

C. $800 profit

D. $800 loss

22. A customer purchases 1 XYZ 60 Call @ $5 and 1 XYZ 60 Put @ $3 when the price of XYZ is trading at $62. If the price of XYZ moves to $52 and the customer exercises the put, what is her profit/loss?

A. $0

B. $300 profit

C. $800 loss

D. $800 profit

23. Use the following information for the question below:

Zee	ACME	FADSLD	DDE
10.00	7s30	10.000s40	4s15s

How many shares of DDE were traded?

A. 4

B. 40

C. 400

D. 4,000

24. A customer sells 1 MNO $40 Call @ $3 and 1 MNO 40 Put @ $6 when the price of MNO is trading at $34. If the price of MNO moves to $30 and the customer receives an exercise notice, what is her profit/loss?

A. $100 loss

B. $300 profit

C. $300 loss

D. $900 profit

25. An RR who has limited trading authorization in a client's account may do which of the following?

A. Deduct a monthly fee for handing the account.

B. Buy and sell stocks, bonds, warrants, and mutual funds.

C. Transfer securities in and out of the client's account.

D. Pay money to a third party.

26. A customer sells 1 MNO $40 Call @ $3 and 1 MNO 40 Put @ $6 when the price of MNO is trading at $34. The maximum gain for this position is:

A. $300

B. $400

C. $600

D. $900

27. In early April, a customer sells 1 GCS July 40 listed call for $4 per share and buys 1 GCS October 40 listed call for $6 per share. Prior to expiration, the customer executes closing transactions by purchasing the July 40 call for $7 per share and selling the October 40 call for $8 per share. The profit or loss to the customer is:

A. $100 profit

B. $100 loss

C. $300 profit

D. $300 loss

28. The Securities Act of 1933 pertains to which securities market?

A. primary

B. secondary

C. third

D. fourth

29. A customer with no other securities positions sells 1 ABC October 25 put for a premium of $2, when the price of ABC stock is $25 per share. If the writer is assigned an exercise notice and sells the ABC stock for $22 per share, what is the resulting profit or loss?

A. $100 profit

B. $100 loss

C. $200 profit

D. $200 loss

30. A customer with no other securities positions sells 1 ABC October 25 put for a premium of $2, when the price of ABC stock is $25 per share. What is the maximum profit the writer could realize?

A. $200

B. $2,300

C. $2,500

D. an unlimited amount

31. A customer with no other securities positions sells 1 ABC October 25 put for a premium of $2, when the price of ABC stock is $25 per share. What is the maximum loss the writer could sustain just before expiration?

A. $200

B. $2,300

C. $2,500

D. $2,700

32. A customer with no other securities positions sells 1 ABC October 25 put for a premium of $2, when the price of ABC stock is $25 per share. The day before expiration, what is the stock price per share at which the writer will break even?

A. $23

B. $25

C. $27

D. $29

33. A trade for 325 shares may be settled by all of the following deliveries, EXCEPT:

A. 325 certificates, one share each

B. three certificates for 70 shares each, three for 30 shares each, and one for 25 shares

C. four certificates for 80 shares each and one certificate for 5 shares

D. one certificate for 300 shares, one certificate for 10 shares, and three certificates for 5 shares each

34. A convertible bond is issued with a conversion ratio of 10 that it is convertible into common stock selling in the market for $125 a share. What is the parity price of the bond?

A. $1,000

B. $1,250

C. $1,500

D. $1,750

35. Which two of the following items represent ownership in a company?

I. Preferred stock

II. First mortgage bond

III. Common stock

IV. Collateral trust bonds

A. I and II

B. I and III

C. III and IV

D. II and IV

36. To which of the following does the FINRA 5% policy apply?

I. A security sale to a customer from the firm's inventory

II. A trade where the broker acted as agent

III. The sale of a mutual fund to a customer

IV. A trade that took place on the NYSE

A. I only

B. I and II

C. I, II and III

D. I, II, III and IV

29. A customer with no other securities positions sells 1 ABC October 25 put for a premium of $2, when the price of ABC stock is $25 per share. If the writer is assigned an exercise notice and sells the ABC stock for $22 per share, what is the resulting profit or loss?

   A. $100 profit
   B. $100 loss
   C. $200 profit
   D. $200 loss

30. A customer with no other securities positions sells 1 ABC October 25 put for a premium of $2, when the price of ABC stock is $25 per share. What is the maximum profit the writer could realize?

   A. $200
   B. $2,300
   C. $2,500
   D. an unlimited amount

31. A customer with no other securities positions sells 1 ABC October 25 put for a premium of $2, when the price of ABC stock is $25 per share. What is the maximum loss the writer could sustain just before expiration?

   A. $200
   B. $2,300
   C. $2,500
   D. $2,700

32. A customer with no other securities positions sells 1 ABC October 25 put for a premium of $2, when the price of ABC stock is $25 per share. The day before expiration, what is the stock price per share at which the writer will break even?

   A. $23
   B. $25
   C. $27
   D. $29

33. A trade for 325 shares may be settled by all of the following deliveries, EXCEPT:

   A. 325 certificates, one share each
   B. three certificates for 70 shares each, three for 30 shares each, and one for 25 shares
   C. four certificates for 80 shares each and one certificate for 5 shares
   D. one certificate for 300 shares, one certificate for 10 shares, and three certificates for 5 shares each

34. A convertible bond is issued with a conversion ratio of 10 that it is convertible into common stock selling in the market for $125 a share. What is the parity price of the bond?

   A. $1,000
   B. $1,250
   C. $1,500
   D. $1,750

35. Which two of the following items represent ownership in a company?

I.	Preferred stock
II.	First mortgage bond
III.	Common stock
IV.	Collateral trust bonds

   A. I and II
   B. I and III
   C. III and IV
   D. II and IV

36. To which of the following does the FINRA 5% policy apply?

I.	A security sale to a customer from the firm's inventory
II.	A trade where the broker acted as agent
III.	The sale of a mutual fund to a customer
IV.	A trade that took place on the NYSE

   A. I only
   B. I and II
   C. I, II and III
   D. I, II, III and IV

37. A city issuing bonds would retain the services of what type of attorney to issue a legal opinion?

   A. city attorney

   B. district attorney

   C. trust attorney

   D. bond counsel

38. You wish to see an indication of the performance of a revenue bond that matures in 30 years. You would look in:

   A. Bond Buyer's 20 Bond Index

   B. Bond Buyer's 30 Bond Index

   C. Revenue Bond Index

   D. Visible Supply

39. A customer (with no securities positions) sells 1 ABC September 30 put for a premium of $3, when the price of ABC stock is $30 per share. What is the customer's maximum profit?

   A. $3

   B. $30

   C. $300

   D. unlimited

40. A customer owns 100 shares of ABC Corp trading for $90 per share. If company were to declare a 3 for 1 stock split, which of the following statements would be correct?

I.	The customer would own 33 shares.
II.	The customer would own 300 shares.
III.	The shares would be worth $270 per share.
IV.	The shares would be worth $30 per share.

   A. I and III

   B. I and IV

   C. II and III

   D. II and IV

41. Which of the following would be quoted as 5.10% Bid - 5.00% Ask?

   A. treasury bills

   B. treasury notes

   C. treasury bonds

   D. treasury receipts

42. All of the following can be performed by a customer with excess equity in a margin account, EXCEPT:

   A. 100% of the SMA

   B. two times the SMA

   C. three times the SMA

   D. securities equal to two times the SMA

43. What is cash flow?

   A. gross income less operating expenses and mortgage costs

   B. gross income less depreciation plus mortgage costs

   C. gross income plus depreciation plus operating expenses

   D. net income less operating expenses, mortgage costs and depreciation

44. ERISA provides protection for which of the following?

   A. employees from improper investment decisions made by their employers

   B. employees who are not covered by under SIPC

   C. government and public service employees from improper investment decisions by portfolio manager

   D. portfolio managers from the consequences of their improper investment decisions

45. Which of the following statements is (are) correct regarding a trust indenture?

I.	It is required by the Securities Exchange Act of 1934.
II.	It is required by the Trust Indenture Act of 1939.
III.	A trustee must be appointed to act in the interest of the bondholders.

   A. I and III

   B. I and II

   C. II and III

   D. I, II, and III

46. A customer looking for an investment maturing in ten years would choose which of the following?

    A. treasury bonds

    B. treasury notes

    C. treasury bills

    D. treasury STRIPs

47. A firm looking to open a cash account for a corporation requires which of the following documents in order to open the account?

I.	Corporate resolution
II.	Corporate charter
III.	Corporate by-laws

    A. I only

    B. II and III

    C. I and III

    D. I, II, and III

48. What types of securities are listed in the yellow sheets?

    A. the name of market makers and their quotes for over-the-counter (OTC) common stocks

    B. the name of market makers and their quotes for over-the-counter (OTC) corporate bonds

    C. the names of market makers and their quotes for NYSE listed stocks

    D. municipal bonds

49. A customer enters an immediate order to buy stock at the best available price without specifying that price. This describes what type of order?

    A. limit order

    B. stop order

    C. market order

    D. stop-limit order

50. When will an owner in a GNMA pool receive a pass-through of interest and principal?

    A. monthly

    B. quarterly

    C. semi-annually

    D. annually

51. Which of the following statements are correct regarding the resignation of a registered representative from a broker/dealer?

I.	The resignation must be sent to the Board of Governors of the FINRA
II.	The resignation must be sent to the SEC
III.	The resignation must be sent within 30 days
IV.	The resignation must be sent within 60 days

    A. I and III

    B. I and IV

    C. II and III

    D. II and IV

52. Under which of the following circumstances does a DK notice not have to be sent?

    A. when a discrepancy is discovered between the trade and settlement date

    B. when the trade confirmations exchanged between dealers show different securities

    C. when a broker/dealer fails to send a confirmation to the contra broker/dealer

    D. when a broker/dealer sends an erroneous confirmation to a customer

53. A customer wishes to sell 10 uncovered XYZ June 40 calls @ 4-3/4 when the underlying stock is trading at 42. What is the customer's maximum gain?

    A. $4750

    B. $3525

    C. $2750

    D. $2000

54. A broker/dealer is permitted to charge a commission and a markup on the same trade under what circumstances?

   A. if disclosed to the customer

   B. through the consent of the customer

   C. under the permission of the Exchange or the FINRA

   D. under no circumstances

55. Which of the following option positions is (are) considered to be bullish?

I.	Long call
II.	Short call
III.	Long put
IV.	Short put

   A. I only

   B. III only

   C. II and III

   D. I and IV

56. General Manufacturing is offering new shares to the public through a rights offering. The existing shares are trading at $30 per share (ex-rights) and the offering has a subscription price of $29 per share. The corporation is offering 200,000 new shares and has 1,000,000 shares already outstanding. What is the value of the right?

   A. $0.20

   B. $0.25

   C. $0.40

   D. $0.50

57. Of what does the OTC market consist?

   A. trades in securities listed on exchanges

   B. anyone making an offer or bid in the market

   C. institutional investors that deal directly with other institutional investors

   D. broker/dealers that negotiate securities trades not listed on an exchange

58. What is the formula for a short margin account?

   A. credit balance minus short market value equals equity

   B. credits balance plus equity equals short market value

   C. short market value minus credit balance equals equity

   D. credit balance plus short market value equals equity

59. Which of the following guaranties are provided in a variable annuity?

   A. fixed number of dollar payments each month for life of the annuitant

   B. lifetime income that is based on a fluctuating value of a fixed number of units each month

   C. payments of a fixed number of dollars each month for a pre-determined term of years

   D. payments that are based on a fixed value of a fluctuating number of accumulation units each month

60. Which of the following statements is (are) correct concerning mutual funds?

I.	The maximum sales charge is 8%.
II.	A reduced sales charge is available to an investor who signs a letter of intent to purchase a certain amount of shares over a 12-month period.
III.	Under rights of accumulation, purchasers of shares are entitled to a reduced sales charge on new purchases when a breakpoint is reached.
IV.	No load funds may charge a liquidation fee.

   A. I only

   B. III only

   C. III and IV

   D. I, II and IV

61. Which of the following should a registered representative not advise for a customer who wishes to purchase an income bond?

    A. These bonds are typically issued by companies that are involved in bankruptcy proceedings.

    B. The interest on these bonds will be cumulative.

    C. There is a risk that the corporation may not generate enough earnings to make the interest and principal payments.

    D. The interest on these bonds is paid "when, as and if earned".

62. Which of the following information must appear on a trade confirmation?

    | I. | The capacity in which the firm acted (either as broker or dealer) |
    | II. | Amount of commission earned |
    | III. | Time of the trade |
    | IV. | The name of the contra-party to the trade |

    A. I only

    B. II and III

    C. I and II

    D. I, II, III, and IV

63. A registered representative wishing to send a letter to a potential customer regarding a security recommended in a telephone conversation must receive the permission of whom?

    A. NYSE

    B. SEC

    C. branch office manager

    D. no prior approval is required

64. What is the third market?

    A. involves direct trades between individual investors

    B. involves trades in listed securities that occur on the NYSE

    C. involves direct trades between institutional investors

    D. involves trades in listed securities that occur over-the-counter

65. Which of the following statements are TRUE about REITs?

    A. Must distribute at least 90% of their net investment income as dividends.

    B. No less than 60% of their gross income must be derived from real estate investments.

    C. REITs are open-end investment companies.

    D. REITs are limited partnerships.

66. Under the Investment Company Act of 1940, which of the following is NOT considered to be a "management" company?

    A. a no-load open-end mutual fund

    B. a diversified closed-end mutual fund

    C. a non-diversified open-end front load mutual fund

    D. a unit investment trust (UIT)

67. Which of the following activites is not permitted by a municipal securities representative?

    A. offer customers new issues of municipal securities

    B. provide advice to municipal securities issuers

    C. make a purchase of municipal securities for own account

    D. provide advice to customers regarding investments

68. If a customer calls a registered representative and requests that the firm not send reports to their home due to their leaving the country, the firm may hold these reports for how long?

    A. 30 days

    B. 60 days

    C. 90 days

    D. until the customer returns to the country

69. The State of Michigan issues bonds to be used to build a toll bridge. The issue will be considered moral obligation bonds. The resulting bridge is unable to generate revenue that is adequate to pay the principal and interest payments to the bondholders. What action (if any) may be taken on behalf of the bondholders to receive their payments?

A. special assessment by the municipality

B. administrative actions

C. judicial action by the bondholders

D. legislative apportionment

70. The sequence of disclosures in a real estate limited partnership offering are governed under what guidance?

A. Securities Act Industry Guide 4

B. Securities Act Industry Guide 5

C. Securities Act Industry Guide 6

D. Securities Act Industry Guide 7

71. What is the intrinsic value of a call with a strike price of $50 purchased at $4 when the market price of a stock is $52?

A. $200

B. $400

C. $600

D. $800

72. A shareholder who has issued a rights offering has what kind of stock?

A. common

B. preferred

C. prior preferred

D. non-convertible preferred

73. A customer enters an order for the purchase of eight corporate bonds trading on the NYSE. This trade may be executed without first attempting to fill the order on the floor if:

A. written permission from the NYSE is obtained

B. the firm believes it can get a better price in a different marketplace

C. An unsolicited request is given from the customer to do the trade in another marketplace

D. Under no circumstances

74. What is the minimum maintenance requirement under NYSE rules when selling short 1,000 shares of a stock at $8 per share?

A. 30% of market value

B. 100% of market value

C. $2.50 per share

D. $5.00 per share

75. Fluctuations with the value of an annuity unit of a variable annuity contract will correspond most closely with fluctuations in the:

A. inflation

B. Standard & Poor's index

C. the value of securities held in the separate account

D. Dow Jones Industrial Average index

76. An investor who redeems mutual fund shares would receive a payment that is based upon:

A. public offering price

B. bid price on the day the shares are received

C. bid price computed on the day after the shares are received

D. public offering price on the day the shares are received

77. What is the type of bond that a customer buys, which is issued by a railroad and is collateralized by railroad cars?

A. revenue bond

B. mortgage bond

C. equipment trust certificate

D. special situation bond

78. XYZ Securities is owned by General Conglomerate Corp (GCC). A registered representative of XYZ Securities sells 100 shares of GCC to a public customer. This would be considered:

A. in violation of FINRA Conduct Rules

B. a control relationship that must be disclosed to the customer

C. permissible as long as the customer gives written permission before the order is placed

D. no special considerations required in this circumstance

79. A customer enters an order to purchase stock at a price of $15 per share. The trade report is given to the registered representative that the stock was bought at $14.50, which is then relayed to the customer. The next day, it is discovered that the trade was actually executed at $15 per share. What price must be paid for the stock and by whom?

A. The firm must sell the stock to the customer at $14.50 due to the error.

B. The registered representative must absorb the loss and pay $15 for the stock.

C. The customer must pay $15 per share for the stock.

D. The Exchange that executed the trade will absorb the loss in their escrow account, upon application by the firm.

80. What is the difference between NASDAQ Level II and NASDAQ Level III service?

A. Level III permits market makers to change their quotes.

B. Level II permits market makers to change their quotes.

C. Level III shows the firms that are market makers.

D. Level II indicates the inside market.

81. A state wishes to issue a bond for an infrastructure project for which users will pay tolls that will be used to pay off the bond issue. This type of bond is known as:

A. revenue bond

B. general obligation bond

C. debenture

D. corporate bond

82. What are Collateralized Mortgage Obligations (CMOs) commonly known as?

A. REMICs

B. HMOs

C. Sallie Maes

D. REITs

83. A customer wants to sell a security in their possession. What should the registered representative ascertain with respect to the security?

I. Location of the security

II. Whether the security is in deliverable form

III. If the security will be delivered within 3 business days

IV. If the security will be delivered by the 10th business day after the settlement date

A. I and II

B. I, II and IV

C. II and IV

D. I, II, and III

84. Which of the following constitutes a good delivery?

A. over delivery of stock

B. partial delivery of stock

C. bonds that are mutilated

D. bonds that have mutilated coupons

85. The City of Chicago sold revenue bonds two years ago with a 10% coupon that are not callable for five years. Interest rates have declined to 6%, and the city feels that they are likely to increase in the coming years. The city would most likely:

A. refund the bonds on the call date

B. pre-refund the bonds

C. call the bonds immediately

D. both B and C

86. How long is Form 144 effective?

A. 30 days

B. 60 days

C. 90 days

D. when the securities are sold

87. ACME Manufacturing has 5,000,000 shares authorized with 2,000,000 shares issued and 1,500,000 shares outstanding. Which of the following statements are true?

> I. The corporation may issue more shares.
>
> II. The corporation has 500,000 votes.
>
> III. The corporation has 500,000 shares of treasury stock.

A. III only

B. I and III

C. II and III

D. I, II, and III

88. What would the common stock of an automobile maker be considered?

A. emerging growth

B. cyclical

C. defensive

D. special situation

89. Quantity discounts on the purchase of mutual fund shares are available to customers for all of the following EXCEPT:

A. individuals

B. investment club

C. trustees

D. custodian over a minor's custodial account

90. If the IRS determines that a limited partnership is abusive, which of the following may occur?

> I. An additional tax will be levied on the investors
>
> II. Tax deductions will be disallowed
>
> III. Interest will be assessed on the amount tax liability underpaid
>
> IV. Investors may be subject to additional penalties

A. I and II

B. III and IV

C. I, II, and IV

D. I, II, III and IV

91. A customer wishes to withdraw their vested interest in a corporate retirement plan by lump sum and place the money into an IRA. Under the rules for IRA rollovers, when would the proceeds need to be rolled over into the IRA before incurring a tax penalty?

A. 30 days

B. 60 days

C. 90 days

D. 1 year

92. If the bid price of an open-end fund is $15 per share and the asked price is $16 per share, what is the fund's sales charge percentage?

A. 6.00%

B. 6.25%

C. 8.00%

D. 8.50%

93. A customer purchased an 8% corporate bond at 92 with a maturity of 20 years. What is the yield to maturity?

A. 7.92%

B. 8.75%

C. 8.26%

D. 9.13%

94. A securities firm acting as consultant to ACME Mfg Corp has received a copy of a list with the company's shareholders. What is the securities firm permitted to do with this information?

A. The firm may use this list for prospecting new customers.

B. The firm may use this list for prospecting only with ACME Mfg Corp's written permission.

C. The firm is not permitted to use the list of shareholder's names.

D. The firm is permitted to rent this list to other disinterested parties.

95. A registered rep inputs a customer's data for a variable annuity program on the computer to show the customer hypothetical results over a contract's life on a computer screen. What rate of return assumptions must the screen result use, according to FINRA rules?

A. A zero percent and a maximum rate of 12% must be used; any rate in between 0% and 12% may be used.

B. A zero percent rate must be used, and any other rates up to a maximum of 12% provided that the largest rate used is reasonable in relationship to the market and available investment options.

C. Rates of return would not be dictated by the FINRA for the personalized screen presentation.

D. A zero percent rate must be used, but any other rates may be used as long as the maximum rate is a reasonable expectation of market conditions and investment options available.

96. An ADR represents ownership in which of the following?

A. foreign securities traded in U.S.

B. foreign securities traded overseas

C. U.S. securities traded in overseas

D. U.S. securities traded in the U.S.

97. What is the underlying asset for Sallie Mae?

A. conventional mortgages

B. student loans

C. VA mortgages

D. FHA mortgages

98. The best price available for General Automation's stock is currently $25 per share, which is offered by Firm ABC. Firm XYZ has an order for the stock from a customer. Firm XYZ calls Firm ABC and asks that firm to purchase the security. This is an example of:

A. hypothecation

B. interpositioning

C. backing away

D. front-running

99. Which of the following would be a good delivery for 500 shares?

I.	one certificate worth 500 shares
II.	5-100 share certificates
III.	5-90 share certificates and 5-10 share certificates
IV.	5-60 share certificates and a 200-share certificate

A. I and II

B. I only

C. I, II and III

D. I, II, III, and IV

100. If a city that has sold revenue bonds to finance the construction of a toll bridge experiences a collapse of the bridge during construction, what call provision would the city invoke?

A. catastrophe call

B. defeasance call

C. sinking fund call

D. disaster call

101. If the initial transaction in a margin account is the purchase of 100 shares of a security at $16 per share, what is the NYSE minimum margin?

A. $2,000

B. $1,600

C. $1,000

D. $800

102. The goals of limited partnerships under the Tax Reform Act of 1986 emphasize:

A. tax shelter

B. income

C. depreciation

D. tax credits

103. Which of the following is not considered a characteristic of a defined benefit plan?

A. plan may be adopted by a company for a key employee nearing retirement age

B. annual benefit received is non-taxable

C. annual contributions may vary

D. annual benefit received in retirement is fixed

104. An investor owns a 10% bond (Bond A) and 12% bond (Bond B). New issue bonds have an interest rate of 11%. All of the following are true EXCEPT:

A. The investor will be able to sell Bond A for $1,100.00.

B. Bond B has increased in value and can be sold at a premium.

C. Bond A has decreased in value and can be sold at a discount.

D. When interest rates go up, bond prices go down.

105. What may be used to purchase a mortgage used to finance housing for the elderly or urban renewal?

A. GNMA

B. FNMA

C. FHLB

D. FINRA

106. Each of the following associates of an NYSE member firm needs the employer's permission to open a margin account EXCEPT:

A. secretary of another NYSE member firm

B. registered representative of another NYSE member firm

C. bank teller

D. president of the bank

107. DEF Corp is listed on the NYSE. XYZ Securities sells 100 shares of DEF to a customer from its own account. If this trade is not executed on the floor of an exchange, it must be reported:

A. within 90 seconds of the trade taking place

B. on the day of the trade (T+0)

C. within five business days after the trade takes place (T+5)

D. within seven business days after the trade takes place (T+7)

108. When is payment for the regular-way purchase of a round lot of U.S. Treasury notes and bonds due?

A. trade day

B. following business day

C. the 5th business day after the trade date

D. the 7th business day after the trade date

109. Who has the primary enforcement responsibility of MSRB regulations over a company that decides to form a subsidiary for the purpose of selling municipal bonds?

A. FINRA

B. SIPC

C. NYSE

D. MSRB

110. A customer, in a cash account, purchases 1 DEF 60 Put @ $2 and sells 1 DEF 70 Put @ $6 when the price of ABC stock is trading at $63. Which of the following best describes the position's strategy?

I.	bearish
II.	bullish
III.	debit
IV.	credit

A. I and III

B. II and IV

C. I and IV

D. II and IV

111. A broker/dealer is required to provide open disclosures to customers in all of the following situations EXCEPT:

A. the amount of commission earned in an agency transaction

B. whether the firm is acting as a broker or dealer

C. the firm's inventory position

D. the interest rate charged on margin debt balances

112. Funds held in a sinking fund may be used for all of the following purposes EXCEPT:

    A.   redeem the bonds at maturity

    B.   exercise a partial call

    C.   pay a dividend to bondholders

    D.   repurchase bonds in open market

113. What is a workable indication on a block of municipal bonds?

    A.   a bond bid

    B.   a bid price that is likely

    C.   a bond offering

    D.   a quote for both the bid and offered side of the market

114. Which of the following is required to register as an investment advisor?

    A.   broker/dealers

    B.   banks

    C.   a publisher of an investment newsletter

    D.   a general circulation newspaper

115. What is program trading?

    A.   only available to small investors

    B.   not allowed by the NYSE

    C.   used for money management

    D.   known as computer-aided trading

116. Which of the following acts pertain to Investment Companies?

    | I. | Securities Act of 1933 |
    | II. | Investment Company Act of 1940 |
    | III. | Investment Advisers Act of 1940 |

    A.   I and II

    B.   I, II, and III

    C.   I only

    D.   II only

117. A competitive sale of a new issue municipal bond will result in the acceptance of bids through all of the following EXCEPT:

    A.   auction

    B.   seal

    C.   oral

    D.   notice of Sale

118. An investor looking to purchase bonds used to finance the building of a sports arena should analyze all of the following EXCEPT:

    A.   the existence of a competing facility

    B.   debt per capita

    C.   the coverage

    D.   the area's population

119. A specialist's book shows the inside market for an issue of 10.75 Bid / 11 Ask. What is the specialist allowed to do?

    | I. | Purchase the stock for 10.88 for his own account. |
    | II. | Sell the stock for 11 from his own account. |
    | III. | Permitted to charge an odd lot differential for an odd lot trade. |
    | IV. | Match a market order with a limit order on the book. |

    A.   I and III

    B.   II only

    C.   I, III and IV

    D.   I, II, III, and IV

120. When do listed options that are expiring cease trading?

    A.   at 2 p.m. Central time; 3 p.m. Eastern time on the business day prior to expiration date

    B.   at 2 p.m. Central time; 3 p.m. Eastern time on the expiration date

    C.   at 3 p.m. Central time; 4 p.m. Eastern time on the business day prior to expiration date

    D.   at 3 p.m. Central time; 4 p.m. Eastern time on the expiration date

121. Three firms are participating in the underwriting of a bond issued by a municipality. A customer wishes to purchase one of these bonds but wants an official statement first. Securities firm A does not have to give an official statement to the customer, provided that:

   A. Securities firm A is the managing underwriter.

   B. The customer is deemed a sophisticated investor.

   C. The municipality uses a competitive bid process to form the underwriting syndicate.

   D. The municipality does not provide an official statement.

122. A municipal securities representative receives an order from a customer, which the representative believes is not suitable for the customer, and advises the customer such but the customer insists on the trade. What should the representative do?

   A. execute the order after obtaining approval of the firm's municipal securities principal

   B. execute the order with approval from the MSRB

   C. not execute the order

   D. execute the order

123. What must an issuer that plans to offer $800,000 of securities in multiple states do?

   A. The securities do not need to be registered with the SEC.

   B. The securities must be registered with the SEC.

   C. FINRA firms would not be permitted to participate in the offering.

   D. The SEC will disallow the offering.

124. A customer enters a limit order to buy XYZ at $40 per share. Which of the following price executions would be acceptable?

I.	$39.75
II.	$39.95
III.	$40.00
IV.	$40.10

   A. III only

   B. III and IV

   C. I, II and III

   D. I, II, III, and IV

125. From which party can a municipal security not be purchased from in the secondary market?

   A. a broker's brokers

   B. dealers

   C. issuers

   D. customers

126. Which of the following municipal bonds would have the greatest increase in price when interest rates fall?

   A. discount bond maturing in 1 year

   B. premium bond maturing in 1 year

   C. discount bond maturing in 20 year

   D. premium bond maturing in 20 year

127. Of the following, who may not trade for his own account?

   A. a registered options trader

   B. a floor broker

   C. a market maker

   D. a competitive options trader

128. Which of the following purchase would have the lowest degree of risk to capital?

   A. common stocks

   B. options

   C. corporate bonds

   D. warrants

129. What would be the exact settlement date when a syndicate accepts the last purchase order for a municipal issue?

   A.   5 business days (T+5)

   B.   7 business days (T+7)

   C.   30 calendar days (T+30)

   D.   cannot be determined

130. When purchasing a general obligation municipal bond, which of the following would be considered by the investor?

   I.   the direct and any overlapping debt per capita

   II.   the ratio of assessed value to estimated value

   III. the issuer's tax collection records

   IV.   trends in assessed valuation

   A.   I only

   B.   I, II and III

   C.   II and III

   D.   I, II, III, and IV

131. Which of the following are not found on the floor of the NYSE?

   A.   registered representatives

   B.   floor brokers

   C.   specialists

   D.   competitive traders

132. Which of the following is required when a customer requests that a registered representative exercise discretion in an account?

   I.   approval of the firm

   II.   signed trading authorization by the customer

   III. a completed customer account form

   A.   I only

   B.   I and II

   C.   II and III

   D.   I, II, and III

133. What is a municipal securities firm required to do when receiving an order from a customer?

   A.   The firm is required to make a reasonable effort to obtain a fair and reasonable price.

   B.   The firm must contact at least three market makers in the issue.

   C.   The firm must execute the order at exactly its fair market value.

   D.   The firm must obtain a fair and reasonable price.

134. Which of the following individuals would be considered an insider?

   I.   corporate officer

   II.   corporate director

   III. 10% or more holder of stock in the corporation

   IV.   10% or more holder of bonds in a corporation

   A.   I only

   B.   I and II

   C.   I, II, and III

   D.   I, II, III, and IV

135. What type of order does a customer enter to sell 100 shares of common stock @ $25 per share?

   A.   a market order

   B.   a limit order

   C.   a stop order

   D.   a stop limit order

136. A customer purchased a Mar 30 put on ABC stock and also purchased a Mar 30 call on A6C stock. This position is known as a:

   A.   long straddle

   B.   vertical spread

   C.   short straddle

   D.   option spread

137. Which of the following statements are not correct about municipal securities trading in the secondary market?

  A. Municipal securities trade over-the-counter (OTC).

  B. Municipal securities may be listed on the NASDAQ.

  C. The largest participants are institutional investors.

  D. Most trades are performed on a dealer basis.

138. A feasibility study performed on a bond issue used to finance a toll road determines sufficient coverage. This includes:

  A. The facility has the ability to meet its operating costs.

  B. The facility has the ability to generate sufficient revenues.

  C. The facility has the ability generate a profit.

  D. both A and B

139. Which of the following will be true when a firm receives an order to sell 1,000,000 shares of stock?

I.	It will be executed on the exchange floor.
II.	Execution will take place in the third markets.
III.	The buyer will initiate the sale.
IV.	The transaction is a secondary distribution.

  A. I and III

  B. I and IV

  C. II and III

  D. II and IV

140. What is the maximum duration for listed equity options?

  A. 1 month

  B. 3 months

  C. 6 months

  D. 9 months

141. Which of the following is correct concerning copies of account statements for a third-party given power of attorney?

  A. Original copies of statements are sent to the third-party; the customer receives duplicates.

  B. The customer is sent original copies of account statements; the third-party receives duplicates.

  C. Original copies are kept by the registered representative, who sends duplicate copies to both the third party and the customer.

  D. Only the customer receives copies of account statements.

142. On what date do equity options expire?

  A. the last Friday of the expiration month at 2 pm

  B. the third Friday of the expiration month at 2 pm

  C. the Saturday following the last Friday of the expiration month

  D. the Saturday following the third Friday of the expiration month

143. Which of the following are correct concerning oil and gas developmental programs?

I.	The degree of risk is lower than exploratory programs.
II.	They exist to develop existing wells.
III.	Investors returns are normally lower than exploratory programs.
IV.	They are referred to as wildcat programs.

  A. I and III

  B. I and IV

  C. II and III

  D. II and IV

144. Limited partnership agreements must contain each of the following statements EXCEPT:

A. limits on compensation paid to the general partner

B. the rights of limited partners to inspect the books and records of the partnership

C. limits on the general partners right to compete with the partnership

D. the right of limited partners to assign their interest in partnership property

145. Which of the following is correct regarding the responsibilities of a corporate officer?

I. must report any changes in holdings of that company promptly

II. may short sell stock

III. is free to take short term profits in the security without condition or restriction

IV. is not allowed to trade the security under any circumstances

A. I only

B. I and II

C. I, II, and III

D. I, II, III, and IV

146. Which of the following is not an exempt security?

A. securities issued by a bank

B. securities issued by the U.S. government

C. private placement securities

D. municipal securities

147. A registration statement has been filed with the SEC for an offering that has not been released by the Commission. Which of the following would not be considered a violation by a registered representative?

I. The customer is promised an allotment of 500 shares.

II. The registered representative accepts an unsolicited deposit of funds after the customer receives the red herring.

III. The customer is sent a preliminary prospectus.

IV. The registered representative tells the customer that the stock is likely to double within a year.

A. II and III

B. I, II, and III

C. III only

D. I, II, III, and IV

148. Which of the following activities would be considered manipulative?

A. A firm enters a series of buy and sell orders at the same price.

B. Two firms engage in sales to show more trading volume.

C. Painting the tape.

D. All of these activities are considered manipulative.

149. Which of the following activities are permissible under the Securities Act of 1933?

A. Borrowing shares and selling them to a person making a tender offer for the shares.

B. Making a stabilizing bid that does not involve a new issue.

C. A firm may hypothecate a customer's securities to a bank to finance the debit balance.

D. A firm loaning a customer money to purchase a new issue.

150. An investment banker performs which of the following functions?

> I. advises the issuer
>
> II. advises as to the most appropriate type of security for the offering
>
> III. conducts a legal examination of the issuer
>
> IV. examines the financial information of the issuer

A. I and II

B. III and IV

C. I, III, and IV

D. I, II, III, and IV

151. The president of a company, who has 4,000,000 shares outstanding, wishes to sell as many shares as possible. The weekly volume for the stock recently was: (for the weeks ending): February 3-25,000 shares; February 10-30,000 shares; February 17-40,000 shares; February 24-35,000 shares; March 1-30,000 shares. How many shares may the company president sell?

A. 32,000 shares

B. 32,500 shares

C. 33,750 shares

D. 40,000 shares

152. Which of the following statements apply to an investor who has purchased stock through a Regulation D offering and is looking to sell?

A. must sell the shares under Rule 144

B. must hold the securities for two years prior to filing Form 144

C. may sell the shares under Rule 144 after holding them fully paid for one year

D. is exempt from Rule 144 if the shares are held and fully paid for one year

153. What is the order of underwriting fees by size (smallest to largest)?

> I.   underwriter's concession
>
> II. spread
>
> III. selling group concession
>
> IV. reallowances

A. I, III, II, and IV

B. IV, III, I, and II

C. IV, I, III, and II

D. III, I, IV, and II

154. A sell order of 1,000 shares of ABC at the close receives:

A. the closing price of the day

B. a price close to the closing price

C. the bid price at the close

D. the asked price at the close

155. What is the purpose of a redemption notice?

A. redeem a stock issue

B. call a mutual fund

C. call a bond issue

D. provide a statement of fact

156. A document that is a summary of the registration statement and provides information to potential purchasers is different from an advertisement that shows the type of security offered, the price of the security and the names of the underwriters in all of the following EXCEPT:

A. the ability to accept orders based on the document

B. the inclusion of the price of the securities offered

C. when they are used in relation to the effective date

D. the amount of disclosures made

157. A customer enters an order to buy ABC at 55 Stop Limit. After receipt of his order, the following trades occur: 54.75, 54.88, 55, 55.13, and 55. Which of the following statements is (are) correct?

I.	The order is triggered at 55.
II.	The order is triggered at 55.13.
III.	The order is executed at 55.
IV.	The order is executed at 55.13.

A.   I and III

B.   I and IV

C.   II and III

D.   II and IV

158. A specialist will reduce which of the following orders on the ex-dividend date of a stock?

I.	buy stops
II.	sell stops
III.	buy limits
IV.	sell limits

A.   II and III

B.   II and IV

C.   I and II

D.   I, II, III, and IV

159. The FINRA 5% Mark-up Policy applies to a member who acts as:

A.   a distributor in a registered secondary offering

B.   a seller of mutual fund shares to a client

C.   a dealer

D.   part of a selling group in a primary distribution

160. Which of the following is excluded from the definition of sales literature under the FINRA Rules of Fair Practice?

A.   research reports

B.   reprints or excerpts from other advertisements

C.   market letters

D.   tombstone ads

161. A registered representative sold 100 shares of ABC, a new stock issue, to a customer at the offering price of $25 per share. A month later, ABC is selling in the market at $22 bid. If the customer expresses strong concern about the decline in value, what would be correct about a representative's offer to buy 100 shares from the customer at $24 per share?

A.   This would not be considered a violation of FINRA rules.

B.   This would be a violation of FINRA rules against guaranteeing a customer against loss.

C.   This is not a violation of FINRA rules, since the representative will take the loss.

D.   This is a violation of FINRA rules against stabilizing quotes on a new issue.

162. In October, a customer buys 1 XYZ January 30 put @ $4 and sells 1 XYZ January 40 put for $13. At what price would the long option position go in-the-money?

A. $35

B. $30

C. $32

D. $25

163. A straddle writer anticipates which of the following?

A.   a stock price decrease

B.   a stock price increase

C.   no significant movement in the price of the stock in either direction

D.   a substantial movement in the price of the stock either up or down

164. What are hot issues?

A.   securities that sell immediately at a premium over the public offering price in the secondary market

B.   securities that sell immediately at a discount over the public offering price in the secondary market

C.   securities issued that do not change in price over the public offering price in the secondary market

D.   none of the above

165. What is the intrinsic value of an option?

    A. the amount of premium that exceeds the option's in-the-money value

    B. the amount a customer must pay at the close

    C. the amount that the option is in-the-money

    D. the maximum profit

166. Which of the following best describes an oil and gas direct participation program exploratory well?

    A. one that has been drilled in an unproven field and is located away from proven fields

    B. one that has been drilled in close proximity to oil producing wells

    C. a well with a lower return to investors than development wells

    D. one that receives large investment tax credits

167. Which of the following are considered to negative aspects of non-registered limited partnerships?

    I. limited liquidity
    II. limited liability
    III. flow through of tax consequences
    IV. IRS scrutiny of the tax returns of the participants

    A. I and IV

    B. II and III

    C. I, III, and IV

    D. I, II, III, and IV

168. Which of the following are correct in regards to a Regulation A offering?

    I. An affiliate of the issuer may offer $300,000 of the securities.
    II. The offering may not exceed $1,500,000.
    III. A Regulation A offering is exempt from registration .
    IV. The issuer has to file an offering statement with the SEC.

    A. III and IV

    B. II and IV

    C. I and III

    D. I, II, III, and IV

169. A company first sold stock publicly in 1972. In 1977, they repurchased 200,000 shares. Today, they are selling 500,000 shares to the public (200,000 were repurchased in 1977). This is best described as a(n):

    A. initial offering

    B. primary offering

    C. split offering

    D. secondary offering

170. A firm is participating in the underwriting of a new issue not yet released by the SEC. Which of the following can the firm send to its customers?

    A. red herring

    B. research report

    C. A or B

    D. A and B

171. Which of the following statements applies to a firm that has agreed to participate in an underwriting?

I.	The firm may continue market making activities in that security.
II.	The firm may not continue market making activities in that security.
III.	Stabilization may eventually occur on the offering.
IV.	Stabalization may not occur until the offering is completed.

- A. I and III
- B. I and IV
- C. II and III
- D. II and IV

172. A registered representative will inquire about which of the following when deciding on whether an investment is suitable for a customer?

I.	prior investment experience
II.	current tax situation
III.	available financial resources
IV.	investment objectives of the customer

- A. I, II, and III
- B. I, III, and IV
- C. II, III, and IV
- D. I, II, III, and IV

173. A company is selling shares to the public for the first time. Which of the following statements are correct?

I.	The offering is a primary distribution.
II.	The offering is an initial public offering.
III.	The offering is a secondary distribution.
IV.	The offering is a private placement.

- A. I only
- B. II only
- C. I and II
- D. III and IV

174. Which of the following is permitted while Form 144 is being prepared by a firm providing assistance to an affiliated person looking to sell shares?

- A. solicit buy orders to match with sell orders
- B. contact customers that indicated an unsolicited interest in the security within the last 60 days
- C. contact firms that inquired about the security in the last 60 days
- D. all of the above

175. Which of the following is not an activity of an investment banker?

- A. accept time and demand deposits
- B. act as underwriter
- C. purchase securities for its own account
- D. participate in the distribution of new issues

176. A company is offering common stock to the public with the underwriters' concession of $0.80 per share, a selling group concession of $0.50 a share, and a management fee of $0.15 per share. What is the spread?

- A. $0.50
- B. $0.80
- C. $0.95
- D. $1.45

177. An order to buy 400 shares of ABC at $35, immediate-or-cancel, is entered prior to the market opening. The following trades occur in ABC when trading begins: 100 shares at $35, 200 shares at $35, and 100 shares at $35. How many shares did this order receive?

A. 100 shares

B. 200 shares

C. 300 shares

D. 400 shares

178. What is the purpose of a tombstone ad?

A.   redeem a stock issue

B.   call a mutual fund

C.   call a bond issue

D.   provide a statement of fact

179. A customer enters an order to sell at $43 Stop. Where would this order be entered, relative to the market price of the stock?

I.	below the current market price
II.	at the current market price
III.	above the current market price

A.   I only

B.   III only

C.   II and III

D.   I, II, and III

180. An order to buy 50 shares of XYZ stock "at the close" would be executed at what price?

A.   the bid price at the close

B.   the asked price at the close

C.   on the last trade of the day

D.   the next day's opening price because it's for an odd lot order

181. The specialist for a stock has a Good-Till-Cancelled order on the books to purchase @ $40 per share. The next day the stock starts trading without a $0.55 dividend. The limit order on the book would be:

A. $39.45

B. $39.63

C. $39.50

D. $39.38

182. When may a representative buy securities in a customer's account without authorization?

A.   when the broker advises the client's secretary the securities have been purchased

B.   when the broker advises a branch office manager that the securities have been purchased

C.   when the broker enters a stop order and sends a memo to the Compliance Department regarding his actions

D.   when the customer gives the representative discretion as to time and price

183. A registered representative must do which of the following when transacting security business for the personnel of another FINRA firm?

A.   notify the employer member in writing of the opening of the account prior to executing a transaction

B.   send duplicate confirmations and statements of such transactions or accounts

C.   both

D.   neither

184. Which of the following records are a registered representative required to maintain?

I.	securities owned by the client and all subsequent purchases and sales
II.	client positions held by your firm by security name
III.	all client orders placed with the order department (including those subsequently canceled)
IV.	dividends paid to the client on any securities held in the street name

A.   I only

B.   I and II

C.   II and III

D.   I, III, and IV

185. A customer buys 100 shares of ADM @ $30 and sells 1 ADM Oct 30 call @ $8. What is the break even for this position?

    A. $22

    B. $24

    C. $30

    D. $38

186. A customer is long 1 April 40 call. On ex-date of a 2-for-1 stock split, the customer will be long:

    A.   1 April 40 call for 100 shares

    B.   1 April 20 call for 200 shares

    C.   2 April 20 calls for 100 shares each

    D.   2 April 40 calls for 100 shares each

187. Which of the following penalties apply to a registered representative in violation of FINRA's Rules of Fair Practice?

I.	Censure
II.	Fine
III.	Suspension
IV.	Expulsion

    A.   I and III

    B.   II and IV

    C.   I, III, and IV

    D.   I, II, III, and IV

188. Which of the following corporate characteristics is the most difficult for a limited partnership to avoid?

    A.   Perpetuity

    B.   Limited liability

    C.   Centralized management

    D.   Free transferability of interests

189. Which of the following are correct regarding the partnership democracy provisions of a limited partnership agreement?

I.	They are designed to protect the limited partner's investment
II.	The require detailed reports regarding the partnership business operations and provide for the annual meeting
III.	They require a majority rule vote of the limited partners before the investments of the entity can be sold or refinanced
IV.	They define repurchase plans and provide for transferability rules

    A.   I and II

    B.   II and III

    C.   I, II, and III

    D.   I, II, III, and IV

190. Which of the following are deductions from the proceeds of an offering prior to an investment in a DPP project?

I.	Acquisition costs
II.	Selling costs
III.	Offering costs
IV.	Organizational costs

    A.   I and II

    B.   III and IV

    C.   II and III

    D.   I, II, III, and IV

191. Which of the following conditions must be met for an exemption under Rule 147?

> I.   80% of the issuer's business must come from within its own state
>
> II. 80% of the proceeds of the offering must be intra-state
>
> III. 100% of the securities must be sold intra-state
>
> IV. Resales within 9 months of the last sale must be intra-state

A. III only

B. I, II and III

C. III and IV

D. I, II, III, and IV

192. Of the following, which must be included in a registration statement?

> I.   The capitalization of the issuer
>
> II. The general character of the business
>
> III. The use of proceeds of the offering
>
> IV. Any legal proceedings involving the issuer

A. II, III, and IV

B. I, II, and IV

C. I, II, and III

D. I, II, III, and IV

193. General Mfg. Corp. has a new issue in registration. The prospectus shows several promotional pieces to be used with the offering. Upon the effective date, which of the following could be sent to customers?

A. Prospectus

B. Promotional material

C. A or B

D. A and B

194. Which of the following statements applies with regards to the rules about a broker/dealers' use of customers' securities?

> I.   Securities of customers must be segregated from those of the firm
>
> II. Firms have the right to borrow customers' securities
>
> III. Firms may hypothecate customers' securities up to 200% of the debit balance
>
> IV. Firms are not allowed to hypothecate customers' securities under any circumstances

A. I only

B. I and II

C. III only

D. IV only

195. Which of the following investors may be counted as an investor in a Regulation D offering?

> I.   A husband and wife, each holding title separately
>
> II. A person with a net worth of $1,000,000
>
> III. An investment club formed to purchase these securities
>
> IV. An investor with a net worth of $250,000

A. IV only

B. I and II

C. I, II, and IV

D. I, II, III, and IV

196. All of following statements are correct regarding a firm commitment underwriting EXCEPT:

A. The managing underwriter faces risk in the offering

B. The syndicate faces risk in the offering

C. The managing underwriter is also a member of the syndicate

D. The selling group faces risk in the offering

197. A non-affiliated person made a purchase of restricted stock. When may stock be sold without being subject to volume limits?

A. Owned and fully paid for two years

B. Fully paid and owned for one year

C. Held in a margin account for three years

D. Non-affiliated persons are always subject to volume restrictions

198. In technical analysis, a consolidating market has what type of trend line?

A. Exponential

B. Sideways

C. Upwards

D. Downwards

199. A customer enters an order to purchase 1,000 shares of XYZ at 38, Stop 42. A report is received that the customer bought 700 shares at $38 per share. What order will remain on the book?

A. Buy 300 at 38 or buy 1,000 at 42 Stop

B. Buy 300 at 38 or buy 300 at 42 Stop

C. Buy 1,000 at 38 or 300 at 42 Stop

D. The balance is canceled; no order remains

200. What does the notation zr in a New York Stock Exchange Bond quote yield column mean?

A. Convertible bond

B. Deep discount

C. Yield not available

D. Zero coupon

201. Investment Companies are regulated under what securities law?

I.	Securities Exchange Act of 1934
II.	Trust Indenture Act of 1939
III.	Investment Advisers Act of 1940
IV.	Investment Company Act of 1940

A. I, II, III, and IV

B. I, II, and III

C. IV only

D. I only

202. A customer enters an order to sell at 37 stop with the following sequence of trades occurring: 39.5, 39, 38.75, 37.5, 37, and 36.75. Which of the following statements is (are) correct?

I.	The order is triggered at 37
II.	The order is triggered at 36.75
III.	The order is executed at 36.75
IV.	The order is not executed

A. I and III

B. I only

C. II and III

D. I and IV

203. If a customer enters an order to buy 10,000 shares of XYZ at $25 and decides that she can wait until the whole order is filled, this is known as:

A. Immediate-or-cancel

B. Fill-or-kill

C. All-or-None

D. Not held

204. A company's stock closed today on an uptick at $30 per share with the stock going ex-dividend the next day at a $0.70 per share dividend. What is the lowest price at which the stock can be sold short on the opening trade tomorrow?

A. $30.70

B. $30.00

C. $29.38

D. $29.30

205. Which of the following statements are true regarding a registered representative with a limited trading authority over a customer's account?

I.	All orders are subject to frequent review by a delegated individual within the firm
II.	A check and securities may not be issued in the name of the registered representative
III.	Periodic confirmations of the continuance of the trading authority is required
IV.	The registered representative may receive confirmations and statements on the customer's behalf

    A.   I only

    B.   I and IV

    C.   II and III

    D.   II and IV

206. A stock will begin trading ex-dividend on Monday, July 8. On which of the following day(s) can a customer purchase shares of the stock and still be entitled to the dividend?

I.	Friday, July 5 for regular way settlement
II.	Monday, July 8 for regular way settlement
III.	Wednesday, July 10 for cash settlement
IV.	Monday, July 15 for cash settlement

    A.   I or III

    B.   I or IV

    C.   II or III

    D.   II or IV

207. What is the reason that arbitration is a preferred method used in settling disputes in the securities industry over litigation?

    A.   It is often less costly than litigation

    B.   It results in decisions that are more binding than those of local courts

    C.   It excludes those arguments from personnel of firms outside the industry

    D.   It allows the parties with more opportunity to present their cases

208. Which of the following types of option transactions are considered the most speculative?

    A.   Selling a spread position

    B.   Writing an uncovered call

    C.   Holding a call

    D.   Holding a spread position

209. In June, a customer sells 1 DEF September 40 put @ $5 and sells 1 DEF September 40 call for $3, when the price of DEF is @ 38. At expiration, the put is exercised and the stock purchased is sold for 35 while the call expires unexercised. What is the profit or loss on this transaction?

    A. $300 profit

    B. $500 profit

    C. $500 loss

    D. $800 loss

210. Which of the following is the order of priority for settling accounts for a limited partnership that has gone bankrupt?

I.	Unsecured creditors
II.	Secured lenders
III.	Limited partners
IV.	General partners

    A.   II, III, I, IV

    B.   III, II, I, IV

    C.   II, I, III, IV

    D.   II, I, IV, III

211. Which of the following statements describes the management in a real estate limited partnership?

I.	It is responsible for the operations of the properties that are owned by the partnership
II.	It is responsible for delegating the management for each function area
III.	The general partner is the key executive
IV.	It is responsible for selecting properties for investment

- A. I and II
- B. I and IV
- C. II, III, and IV
- D. I, II, III, and IV

212. Where do the deductions primarily come from in the first year of an oil and gas drilling partnership?

- A. Depreciation
- B. Depletion
- C. Intangible drilling costs
- D. Investment tax credits

213. To which of the following offerings does the Securities Act of 1933 apply?

I.	ACME common stock
II.	ACME bonds
III.	City of St. Louis municipal bonds
IV.	A railroad common stock

- A. I, II, and IV
- B. I and II
- C. I only
- D. I, II, III, and IV

214. What best describes the cooling-off period?

- A. The time between the registration filing and the effective date
- B. The date the offering is released by the SEC
- C. The period before the filing of the registration statement
- D. The period before any errors in the prospectus are corrected

215. A customer purchases a security in the secondary market. Under which circumstances will the customer be sent a prospectus?

- A. A secondary distribution has taken place within the past 90 days
- B. The company sold its second issue of the security within the past 90 days
- C. The initial public offering occurred within the past 90 days
- D. Under no circumstances

216. A customer has a balance in an account that can be withdrawn immediately upon request. How often should statements be sent to the customer?

- A. Monthly
- B. Quarterly
- C. Semi-annually
- D. Annually

217. What is the disclosure document is provided with a Regulation D offering?

- A. Offering memorandum
- B. Prospectus
- C. Private placement memorandum
- D. Official statement

218. XYZ Corporation is looking to issue a private placement in order to raise $7,000,000 in capital. How many investors are permitted to participate in this offering?

- A. 35
- B. 35 accredited and any number of non-accredited
- C. 35 non-accredited and any number of accredited
- D. Unlimited

219. A husband owns 15% of a company's shares while the wife owns 5% percent. Which of the following are correct regarding the wife's desire to sell her shares?

I.	The wife must sell the shares under Rule 144
II.	The wife is not considered an affiliated person
III.	The wife is subject to volume limitations
IV.	The wife will not be subjected to volume limitations

A. I only

B. I and III

C. II and III

D. II and IV

220. An underwriting in which the stock issue is canceled if it is not completely sold is called what?

A. Standby

B. Best Efforts

C. All-or-None

D. Internal Commitment

221. Which type of order may be accepted by a specialist?

A. Not held

B. Good-till-canceled

C. Good-through-week

D. Good-through-month

222. What does the notation cv in the New York Stock Exchange Bond quote yield column mean?

A. Convertible bond

B. Deep discount

C. Yield not available

D. Zero coupon

223. A dealer has a 10% participation in a municipal underwriting of $3,000,000. The dealer sells its entire allotment, but $1,000,000 remain unsold. For how many of the unsold bonds is the dealer liable?

A. $0

B. $100,000

C. $200,000

D. $300,000

224. A customer enters an order to sell at 37 stop with the following sequence of trades occurring: 39.5, 39, 38.75, 37.5, 37, and 36.75. If the order was one to sell at 37 stop limit, which of the following statements is (are) correct?

I.	The order is triggered at 37
II.	The order is triggered at 36.75
III.	The order is executed at 36.75
IV.	The order is not executed

A. I and III

B. I only

C. II and III

D. I and IV

225. The following are true of orders using the DOT order execution system EXCEPT:

A. The order goes directly to the specialist

B. Floor brokers' fees are avoided

C. The system can handle any size order

D. The order can be filled directly from the specialist's book

226. A mutual fund has a net asset value of $15.25 and an offering price of $16.50. Which of the following transactions would be permitted under the FINRA Rules of Fair Practice by an FINRA member firm?

> I.   Sell 300 shares of the fund at $16.00 to a non-FINRA member firm
>
> II. Sell 600 shares of the fund at $16.50 to one of the firm's customers
>
> III. Sell 800 shares of fund at $15.25 to another FINRA member firm through a non-FINRA member

- A. I only
- B. II only
- C. I and II
- D. II and III

227. All of the following documents must be made available to customers of FINRA member firms except:

- A. Certificate of Incorporation and Bylaws
- B. Rules of Fair Practice and Code of Procedures
- C. Firm's balance sheet
- D. Firm's income statement

228. For which of the following may an FINRA member firm charge a customer a service fee?

> I.   Collecting monies due a customer (principal or interest)
>
> II. Safekeeping or custody of a customer's securities
>
> III. Handling an exchange or transfer of a customer's securities
>
> IV. Appraising a customer's securities

- A. I and II
- B. I, II, and III
- C. II, III, and IV
- D. I, II, III, and IV

229. Under FINRA rules, which of the following activities of a registered representative requires prior written approval?

> I.   Sending a form letter to the representative's client
>
> II. Delivering a red herring to the customer
>
> III. Execution of an order in an existing discretionary account
>
> IV. Placing an advertisement in the local shoppers guide

- A. I and II
- B. II and III
- C. II, III, and IV
- D. I, II, III, and IV

230. What percentage of the purchase price must a buyer of an option pay?

- A. 25%
- B. 30%
- C. 50%
- D. 100%

231. A customer is limited to the number of option contracts that may be held on the same side of the market with the same underlying security. That maximum number that may be held is:

- A. 2,000
- B. 4,000
- C. 6,000
- D. 8,000

232. Which two of the following positions are spreads?

> I. Long call ABC April 40; short call ABC April 50
>
> II. Long call DEF May 40; short call DEF July 40
>
> III. Long call FMO January 50; long call FMO January 60
>
> IV. Short call XYZ May 40; short call XYZ February 50

- A. I and II
- B. I and IV
- C. II and III
- D. III and IV

233. In May, a customer buys 100 XYZ common stock @ $70 per share and buys 1 XYZ August 70 put @ 4. At expiration, XYZ is selling @ $80 per share, which allows the put to expire worthless while selling the XYZ shares @ 80. What would be the customer's profit or loss?

- A. $400
- B. $600
- C. $1,000
- D. $1,400

234. A customer buys an option and now wishes to liquidate the position by writing an option with the same term as the option previously written. This transaction is called a(n):

- A. Opening sale
- B. Closing sale
- C. Open interest
- D. Closing purchase

235. If a customer buys 100 shares of XYZ common when the current market value is @ $80 and later buys a put, which of the following would be correct?

- A. The customer has created a married put
- B. The customer has established a covered put
- C. The customer is hedging against a price decline
- D. The customer may have an unlimited loss

236. An investor purchases one XYZ June 55 call for 4 when the stock is at 53. If the stock rises to 61 and the investor exercises the call, which of the following is true of the investor?

- A. Own the stock at a cost of $51 per share
- B. $200 profit
- C. $400 loss
- D. Own the stock at a cost of $59 per share

237. Which of the following investors would not experience a loss if the strike price of an option and the market price of the underlying stock remained the same?

> I. Holder of a straddle position
>
> II. Writer of a straddle position
>
> III. Holder of an at-the-money put
>
> IV. Writer of an at-the-money put

- A. I and III
- B. I and IV
- C. II and III
- D. II and IV

238. A customer creates a spread purchasing 1 ABC Aug 70 call @ 10 and selling 1 ABC Aug 80 call @ 4. Under which of the following circumstances will the customer not experience a gain?

- A. The calls expire worthless
- B. The call spread widens
- C. The market price of the underlying stock is at 77 and the option positions are closed at intrinsic value
- D. The customer sells the Aug 70 call for 8 and repurchases the Aug 80 call for 1

239. It is anticipated that an increase in interest rates will happen in the near future. What might you advise the client to do in this scenario?

I.	Buy Treasury note call options
II.	Buy Treasury note put options
III.	Sell Treasury note call options
IV.	Sell Treasury note put options

   A.   I and III

   B.   I and IV

   C.   II and III

   D.   II and IV

240. A customer wishes to sell 10 uncovered XYZ June 40 calls @ 4-3/4 when the underlying stock is trading at 42. What is the customer's maximum loss?

   A. $35,250

   B. $40,000

   C. $44,750

   D.   Unlimited

241. What is the first source of funding for public housing revenue bonds?

   A.   Income derived from rents

   B.   Government backing

   C.   Proceeds from future issues

   D.   Ad valorem taxes

242. A customer wishes to sell 10 uncovered XYZ June 40 calls @ 4-3/4 when the underlying stock is trading at 42. If the customer closed out the options at 2-1/8, what is the gain or loss?

   A. $2,225

   B. $2,625

   C. $4,000

   D. $4,750

243. A customer sold an NYSE index call @ 80. The customer is exercised when the index reaches 87. What would be the amount of cash settlement?

   A. $70

   B. $700

   C. $7,000

   D. $9,700

244. An investment in a limited partnership direct participation program has which of the following disadvantages?

I.	Tax advantages may be altered by Congress
II.	Investors have no say in management
III.	There is no formalized effective secondary market

   A.   III only

   B.   II only

   C.   I and II

   D.   I, II, and III

245. Which of the following is an advantage in an oil and gas drilling limited partnership?

   A.   Liquidity

   B.   Depletion allowance

   C.   Investors have a say in management matters

   D.   Limited risk of capital

246. Which of the following are features of limited partnership tax shelters?

I.	Income write-off
II.	Liability is limited to pro-rata investment share
III.	Control of management
IV.	Flexibility in types of investments available

   A.   I and III

   B.   III and IV

   C.   I, II, and IV

   D.   I, II, III, and IV

247. Which of the following is not a corporate characteristic established by the IRS in determining if an entity should be treated as a partnership or as an association taxable as a corporation?

A. Continuity of life

B. Limited liability

C. Profit

D. Central management

248. Which of the following are advantages associated with direct participation limited partnership offerings?

I.	Flow through of tax consequences
II.	Tax-free income
III.	Limited liability
IV.	Protection against loss of capital

A. I and IV

B. II and IV

C. I and III

D. I, II, and IV

249. Which of the following should be taken into account when evaluating a direct participation program?

I.	Examine its economic viability
II.	Review its adequacy of capital
III.	Compare its rate of return with other direct participation programs
IV.	Review of how well or poorly the general partners have done in the past

A. I and IV

B. II and III

C. III and IV

D. I, II, III, and IV

250. A customer wishes to sell 10 uncovered XYZ June 40 calls @ 4-3/4 when the underlying stock is trading at 42. What is the customer's break even?

A. $35.25

B. $40.00

C. $44.75

D. $46.75

Answer Key: Practice Test #1

1. D.

The trade was at $10.00 per share. The fact that no volume figure is shown indicates that the trades were 100 shares each.

2. C.

This strategy is a bull put spread that creates a credit when the long put is sold for $2 and the short put is sold for $6 ($6 – $2 = $4). The difference between the strike prices ($70 – $60 = $10) less the credit equals the maximum loss. $10 – $4 = $600.

3. C.

For trades of 10,000 shares, zeros are not deleted, but a decimal is used in place of a comma. The answer is 10,000 shares. The letters "SLD" mean that the stock was sold, and the trade was reported out of sequence.

4. D.

The maximum loss is the combined premiums paid ($500/call + $300/put = $800).

5. A.

American style options can be exercised at any time up to its expiration. A call holder (buyer) has the right, but is not obligated to purchase the underlying security at the strike price. When a stock option expires it becomes worthless. The writer (seller) of a put has a bullish outlook on the market and is looking to profit from the premium.

6. B.

The break even for a call (regardless of whether it is bought or sold) is the strike price plus the premium paid. Since the strike price for ABC call is 30, the price would have to be higher than $30 making choice B the only suitable selection.

7. D.

The fundamental value, which is also referred to as the intrinsic value, occurs for a put when the market price is below the strike price. In this example, the market price is $18, which is below the strike price of $20, resulting in an intrinsic value of $2.

8. D.

The maximum profit for the holder of a put is the strike price less the premium paid. Being long the put gives the holder the right to sell the stock at the strike price in a falling (bearish) market. If the market price were to fall to $20, the holder could exercise the put and sell the stock for $2,500 (1 contract = 100 shares) resulting in a profit of $2,500 minus $100 equal $2,400.

9. A.

A put is in-the-money when the market price is below the strike price; a call goes in-the-money when the market price is above the strike price.

10. A.

The maximum potential loss for a put writer is the strike price less the premium received. Since it is a bullish strategy, if the market price of XYZ stock goes to $0, the writer will have to buy the stock from the holder at $35 per share ($3,500) but since she received a premium of $1.25 ($125), her maximum loss would be $3,500 - $125 = $3,375.

11. A.

The maximum gain to the call writer is the premium received and the maximum loss theoretically is unlimited.

12. D.

The ex-dividend date for trades settled in cash is the business day following the record date.

13. C.

Warrants do not have voting rights, as they represent a future intention to purchase new issue shares of the underlying stock. Warrants may be short or long term (unlike stock options) and may cover more or less than 100 shares (when a warrant is exercised, new shares are created whereas an option exercise involves the purchase or exchange or previously issued market shares of the underlying security).

14. C.

You may purchase options on all of the listed securities.

15. A.

This position is a bull call spread where the call with the higher strike price is purchased and the call with a lower strike price is sold, creating a debit of $3 ($300). The debit is the most that the customer can lose in this transaction.

16. B.

If there is no activity in the account, the client can receive quarterly statements. If there is activity, the client receives a monthly statement.

17. B.

This strategy is a bull call spread that creates a debit when the long call is purchased for $7 and the short call is sold for $4 ($7 – $3 = $4).

18. C.

For volumes of 200 through 9900 shares, the tape deletes the zeros. "7s" is 700 shares.

19. A.

The assessed value, rather than the current market value, is used when calculating taxes. It is important to know that a mill is equal to 0.001 or one-thousandth when performing the calculation. Therefore, the taxes are calculated by multiplying the assessed value of the property ($550,000) by 16 by a mill ($550,000 x 16 x 0.001 = $8800).

20. B.

Selling a small amount of an offering to a firm that is not a participant in the selling group would be considered a reallowance.

21. A.

This position is a long straddle where the holder is uncertain of which way the market will move. The most the holder will lose are the premiums paid, which in this example was $800. Since the call is in-the-money, she would exercise the call and let the put expire worthless, resulting in a gain of $1,000 for exercising the call and a loss of $300 in premiums paid for the put for a net profit of $700.

22. A.

The stock's price moved to $52, resulting in the long straddle reaching its downside break-even point (combined premiums paid were $8; strike price - the premiums paid = put break even). The $500 in premiums paid for the call would be a loss, as the position would expire worthless. The $500 gained by exercising the put results in $0 profit or loss.

23. B.

The symbol "ss" indicates stock trading in round lots of 10 shares. This trade was for four lots of ten, or 40 shares.

24. A.

The position is a short straddle. The hope is that the market neither goes up or down, allowing the writer to profit by earning the premiums. Because the price of MNO fell to $30, the put holder (who is now 10 points in-the-money) will issue an exercise notice, forcing the writer to purchase the stock at $40 per share ($4,000). The market value of MNO stock is $30 per share ($3,000) resulting in a loss of $1,000. Premiums of $9 ($900) were received through the sale of the put and the call as a credit so the net loss would be $100 (the call would expire worthless).

25. B.

Limited trading authorization allow the registered representative to buy and sell for the client. The RR cannot withdraw money or securities.

26. D.

The maximum gain on a short straddle is the combined premiums received from the sale of the call and the put. In this example, $300 was received from selling the call and $600 received for selling the put for a total maximum profit of $900.

27. B.

Originally, the customer wrote a July 40 call and received a $4 premium. He bought an October 40 call and paid a $6 premium, which left him minus $2. Prior to expiration, he bought the July 40 call and paid $7 per share. He also sold the October 40 call and received $8 premium per share, resulting in a plus $1 per share. The minus $2 per share from the original transaction plus the $1 per share for the closing transactions equals minus $1 per share times 100 shares equals a $100 loss.

28. A.

The Securities Act of 1933 governs the initial registration and distribution of securities, which is considered the primary market.

29. B.

The writer received $2 per share in premium, but lost $3 per share on the difference between the $22 and the $25, resulting in a loss of $100.

30. A.

If the option is not exercised, the writer will keep the premium of $2 per share, or $200.

31. B.

The put writer must buy the stock at the exercise price of 25. If the price goes to 0, he could lose $2,500 minus the $200 received as a premium, or $2,300.

32. A.

$25 - $2 premium received = $23.

33. C.

Under Section 11361 of the FINRA Uniform Practice Code (UPC), good delivery of stock constitutes the delivery of 100 shares which represents a "round-lot." Any transaction where the number of share is less than or not divisible by 100 would represent an "odd-lot" transaction. Choice C would not represent a good delivery since the issue amounts do not aggregate into 100 shares: 80 + 80 + 80 + 80 = 320 shares; 5 = 5 shares / bad delivery.

34.   B.

To calculate the parity price or conversion value of the convertible bond, take the current market price of the stock times the conversion ratio. $125 × 10 = $1,250.

35.   B.

Stock issued by a corporation represents an equity share of ownership. Corporations are permitted to issue common shares of stock, which have voting rights regarding management decisions of the corporation and preferred stock which are non-voting shares. Preferred shareholders have priority claim on assets in corporate dissolution over common shareholders and receive dividends. Preferred shares are typically held by owners of a private or pre-public corporation. Once a company goes public, these shares are converted (or can be converted) into shares of common.

36.   B.

The 5% policy applies to firm (member) trades made as both principal or as an agent.

37.   D.

A bond counsel provides legal opinion on the issuance of bonds.

38.   C.

The Revenue Bond Index is comprised of 25 revenue bonds with a maturity in 30 years, with a Moody's rating of A1 and S&P rating of A+. Choice A is incorrect as the 20 Bond Index is an index of general obligation (G.O.) bonds; Choice B is incorrect as there is no 30 Bond Index; Choice D is a measurement of the supply of municipal bonds about to be issued within 30 days.

39.   C.

The maximum gain for a short put is the premium received.

40.   D.

The purpose of this split is to bring down the market price of ABC Corp's stock in order to attract new investors. The result of a 3:1 split would be an increase in the number of shares by a factor 3 and a reduction in the share price by one-third. The value of the holding would remain the same ($90 × 100 shares and $30 × 300 shares = $900).

41.   A.

Treasury bills are quoted are shown discount from par whereas other government securities are quoted as a percentage of par in decimal points representing 32nds of a percent.

42.   C.

A customer is permitted to borrow up to two times the value of the available SMA, whether in cash or securities. Choices A, B and D, are correct.

43.   A.

Cash flow, as determined in a direct participation program, is based on the operating expenses and mortgage costs of the program as deducted from gross income.

44.   A.

ERISA, which is the Employee Retirement Income Security Act of 1974, protects the interest of employees from improper investment decisions.

45.   C.

A trust indenture is required under the provisions of the Trust Indenture Act of 1939, requiring that a trustee be appointed to act for the interests of the bondholders.

46.   B.

Treasury notes have a maturity of 10 years.

47.   A.

A cash account for a corporation only requires a corporate resolution in order to open the account.

48.   B.

The yellow sheets provide information about the market makers and their quotes for corporate bonds that are traded OTC.

49.   C.

A market order is executed at the prevailing market price once entered into a trading system.

50.   A.

The interest and principal payments are distributed monthly.

51.   A.

When a registered representative resigns, a notice of resignation must be sent to the FINRA Board of Governors within 30 days of the resignation.

52.   D.

DK notices, which stands for "Don't Know" are used when a discrepancy occurs between broker/dealers; it does not involve customers.

53.   A.

The maximum gain for selling a call is the premium received. In this example, the gain would be $475 × 10 = $4,750.

54. D.

A firm may not act as broker and dealer in the same transaction.

55. D.

Long calls and short puts are considered bullish positions while long puts and short calls are bearish.

56. A.

To determine the value, first calculate the number of rights needed to equal 1 share of common stock, which would be 1,000,000 outstanding divided 200,000 new shares equals 5. Next, take the difference between the ex-right market value and the subscription price and divide it by 5. $30 - $29 / 5 = $0.20.

57. D.

The over-the-counter (OTC) market is a negotiated market between broker/dealers.

58. A.

Credit balance (CB) minus short market value (SMV) equals equity (EQ) in a short margin account.

59. B.

Choices A, C, and D describe the guarantees and characteristics of a fixed annuity, not a variable annuity.

60. C.

The maximum sales charge for mutual fund shares is 8.5% and a Letter of Intent covers an investor's intention to purchase shares in order to qualify for a lower sales charge level must take place within a 13-month period, not 12.

61. B.

Unlike cumulative preferred stock, interest on income bonds is paid when, as, and if earned.

62. C.

A trade confirmation must disclose whether the firm acted as broker or dealer and the amount of commission earned in the trade. The time the trade took place and the contra-party to the trade may be provided upon the request of the customer, but is not required on the trade confirmation.

63. C.

Correspondence prepared by a registered representative must be approved by a branch manager of the firm prior to distribution.

64. D.

Trades in the third market are usually block trades of stocks listed over-the-counter.

65. A.

Real estate investment trusts resemble closed-end investment companies that trade in the secondary market (similar to company stocks). The Internal Revenue Code requires REITs to distribute at least 90% of their net investment income to avoid double taxation and 75% of a REITs income must be from real estate. They are investment trusts, not limited partnerships as there is no direct flow through of losses to the investors.

66. D.

A unit investment trust (UIT) is an investment company share that is unmanaged, therefore not considered a management company under the Investment Company Act of 1940.

67. D.

Advice provided by a "municipal securities registered representative" is limited to municipal securities.

68. C.

Trade confirmations and statements of account may be held for up to 60 days when traveling inside the United States or 90 days while traveling outside the United States.

69. D.

If a locality defaults on their obligation to pay back a moral obligation bond (not backed by the taxing authority or revenues of the issuer), the state's legislature will need to make a special apportionment to back the principal and interest payments to bondholders.

70. B.

The sequence of disclosure for a real estate limited partnership offering are found in Securities Act Industry Guide 5.

71. A.

When a call option goes in-the-money (market price > strike price), the difference between the two results in intrinsic value - $52 minus $50 = $2 intrinsic value (times 100 = $200). Since the premium is $4, subtracting the intrinsic value from the premium gives you the time value ($2).

72. A.

Common stock owners have a preemptive right against dilution of their shares.

73. C.

An order for less than nine corporate bonds that trade on the NYSE must first be presented on the floor of the NYSE unless the customer gives an unsolicited request trade in another marketplace.

74. D.

A quick rule of thumb for stock sold short regarding the NYSE minimum requirement: if the stock sold short trades at a price of $16-5/8 or above, use the NYSE 30% rule. If it is trading at a price that is less than $16-5/8, use the $5 rule.

75. C.

The market value of the separate account determines the value of an annuity unit for a variable annuity.

76. C.

The redemption price received for mutual funds is the bid or NAV, which is computed on the day after the shares have been received.

77. C.

Equipment trust certificates are issued by companies known as common contract carriers collateralized by equipment owned by the company.

78. B.

Because XYZ Securities is under the ownership control of General Conglomerate Corp, this relationship must be disclosed to the client.

79. C.

The customer must pay the execution price of the stock.

80. A.

Although NASDAQ Levels II and III provide the same information, Level III permits market makers to make changes to their quotes.

81. A.

Municipalities (i.e. cities, counties and states) issue revenue bonds that are backed by user fees paid by the users of the facility, such as roads, stadiums, and arenas.

82. A.

Real Estate Mortgage Investment Conduits are what Collateralized Mortgage Obligations are known as.

83. D.

Before accepting the order, the registered representative must ascertain the location of the security, that the security is in a deliverable form, and if the customer will deliver the certificate within three business days after the trade (T+3 = regular-way settlement).

84. B.

A partial delivery is good delivery.

85. C.

The bonds have not reached their call date, so they cannot be called. The city would instead pre-refund the bonds and sell a new issue at the lower interest rate of 6%. The proceeds of the new issue would be placed in an escrow and used to call the older bonds at maturity.

86. C.

Form 144 is effective for 90 days.

87. B.

Because the corporation has 5,000,000 shares authorized, with only 2,000,000 issued (1,500,000 outstanding and 500,000 held in treasury) the corporation can issue up to 3,000,000 more shares.

88. B.

Automobile stocks are considered cyclical stocks because of their dependence on the business cycle.

89. B.

An investment club would not qualify for quantity discounts.

90. D.

A limited partnership that is deemed abusive may be subject to all of the statements.

91. B.

A rollover of assets from an employer-sponsored retirement plan to a Rollover IRA must be accomplished within 60 days in order to avoid incurring a penalty for early withdrawal of funds.

92. B.

Ask (POP) minus Bid (NAV) divided by Ask = Sales Charge %. ($16 - $15) ÷ $16 = 0.0625 or 6.25%.

93. B.

The customer will make $80 ($1,000 * 8%) upon maturity, over a period of 20 years, or an annual interest of $4 per year. The annual interest payment on an 8% bond is $80, so the adjusted interest is $84 ($80 + $4). The customer bought the bond for $920 and it will mature at $1,000, so the average price is $960. The yield to maturity is 8.75% ($84 divided by $960).

94. B.

Because the firm is acting in an advisory relationship to ACME Mfg Corp, any information obtained as a result of this relationship may not be used without prior written permission.

95. B.

A hypothetical illustration of performance for a variable annuity (and other variable insurance contracts) must show a rate of return of 0% and may show any additional return up to a maximum 12%, provided that the rates illustrated are reasonable in relationship to the market and available investment options.

96. A.

American depository receipts (ADRs) is the receipt of shares of a foreign-based corporation held in safe-keeping in the U.S. that trades in the U.S.

97. B.

Student loans are the underlying assets for Sallie Mae (Student Loan Marketing Agency).

98. B.

Firm ABC has engaged in interpositioning or to act as a third party in the transaction on behalf of Firm XYZ's customer.

99. C.

To be considered a good delivery, the certificates have to be able to be aggregated into round lots of 100 shares. Option IV does not meet this criterion.

100. A.

In the event of a bridge collapse during the construction of the bridge, the city would invoke the catastrophe call to use insurance proceeds to pay for the bonds.

101. B.

In a long margin account, the minimum requirement under Reg. T is 50% the long market value or $2,000, which is the initial minimum requirement. In this transaction, the customer would be required to deposit $1,600 or 100% of the long market value (the customer would not be required to deposit more than the value of the securities).

102. B.

The Tax Reform Act of 1986 removed many of the shelter aspects of limited partnership investments, placing a greater emphasis on the pass-through of income.

103. B.

The benefit received from a defined benefit plan in retirement is taxable.

104. A.

When the stated (nominal) yield on a bond is lower than the current yield, the bond is termed a discount bond. When the nominal yield of a bond is higher than the current yield, the bond is trading at a premium. Bond A with a nominal yield of 10% is now trading at a discount to par; conversely Bond B with a nominal yield of 12% is trading at a premium to par. As interest rates rise, market prices (in general) fall.

105. B.

The Federal National Mortgage Association (FNMA or Fannie Mae) engages in the purchase of mortgages to finance programs such as urban renewal and elder housing.

106. D.

Officers of an NYSE member firm (such as a bank president) does not need approval of the employer to open a margin account.

107. A.

Information regarding a trade involving a customer and stock taken from the firm's inventory that does not take place on the floor of an exchange must be reported within ninety seconds of the trade.

108. B.

The settlement for U.S. Treasury bonds and notes is trade date plus 1 business day (T + 1). Corporate and municipal bonds settle regular-way T + 3, the same as common stock. Cash settlement is always the same day.

109. A.

The enforcement of MSRB municipal regulations is overseen by FINRA. The MSRB is a rule-making body only.

110. D.

A short put is a bullish strategy that is profitable when the market rises, creating a credit, which represents the position's maximum gain.

111. C.

The firm's inventory position is not subject to open disclosure requirements.

112. C.

Common stock shareholders, not bondholders, receive dividends.

113. B.

The workable indication represents a likely offering.

114. C.

Broker/dealers, banks, and general circulation newspapers are exempt from the requirements of registration as a registered investment advisor in accordance with the Investment Advisers Act of 1940.

115. D.

Program trading is trading that is performed by computers.

116. A.

Investment Companies are regulated under the provisions of the Investment Company Act of 1940, and are defined as a security, subject to Section 2(a)(1) of the Securities Act of 1933.

117. D.

It is the Notice of Sale that announces the existence of a competitive sale.

118. B.

The bonds used to finance a sport arena would be financed through the receipts and other program fees generated by the facility, making the bonds revenue bonds. Debt per capita is not a consideration for revenue bonds.

119. C.

The specialist is permitted to purchase the stock for the specialist's account at 10.88 if it is higher than the highest bid of any public customer. The specialist may not sell the stock at 11 because a public customer has made an offer on the stock at 11 based on the inside ask price. The specialist is permitted to charge a differential of an eighth of a point ($0.125) on odd lot trades and market orders are often matched to limit orders on the books of the specialist.

120. D.

All listed options stop trading at 3 p.m. Central time (4 p.m. Eastern time) on the date of their expiration.

121. D.

There is no requirement for the issuer to provide an official statement to the members of the underwriting syndicate; most all issuers make the statement available to provide investors with information necessary to evaluate the quality of the issue.

122. D.

Because the municipal securities representative expressed concerns about the suitability of the transaction with the client and the client insisted that the trade take place, the representative should proceed with the execution of the order.

123. A.

Securities offerings that are less than $5,000,000 would be conducted under Reg. A regardless of the number of states the securities will be offered in.

124. C.

A customer would accept an execution that is at or below the limit order, which would be $39.75, $39.90 and $40. The limit order would not be executed is XYZ rose to a price of $40.10.

125. C.

Municipal securities trading in the secondary market may not be purchased from the issuer.

126. C.

Bonds that trade at a discount to par with long maturities will be more susceptible to a decrease in interest rates than a discount bond with a short maturity.

127. B.

A floor broker is only permitted to trade on behalf of his customers and for the accounts of his firm.

128. C.

Of the choices listed, corporate bonds would have the lowest risk to capital (as most debt securities due) and provide the customer with a priority claim on assets upon dissolution of the company during a bankruptcy proceeding.

129. C.

The normal settlement for new municipal securities that have been issued is about 30 days; however the exact settlement day cannot be determined.

130. D.

An investor should consider all of these things before purchasing general obligation municipal bonds.

131. A.

Registered representative are sales representatives of member broker/dealers of the NYSE. A registered representative is not a member of the NYSE and would not be allowed on the NYSE trading floor.

132. D.

Each of the choices listed is required before a registered representative may be permitted to exercise discretion in a customer's account.

133. A.

When an order for municipal securities is received, the firm is required only to make every reasonable effort to obtain a fair and reasonable price.

134. C.

Choices I, II, and III would be considered corporate insiders; an individual who holds convertible bonds of the corporation is not an owner until the bonds are converted into shares of common stock.

135. B.

Because the customer expressed a price ($25) for the purchase of the stock, this would be a limit order.

136. A.

A long straddle position is established when a put and call of the same underlying security are purchased simultaneously with the same expiration and same strike price. A short straddle position is established when a put and call of the same underlying security are sold simultaneously with the same expiration and strike price.

137. B.

Municipal securities trade OTC and are not listed on the NASDAQ.

138. D.

The feasibility study would look at the ability of the project to generate sufficient revenues for bondholders and pay its operating costs.

139. D.

This transaction, known as a secondary distribution, would be too large to execute on the floor of the exchange and would take place instead in the third market.

140. D.

Listed options generally expire in 9 months from the date of issuance.

141. A.

Under a third-party trading authorization, original account statements and trade confirmations are sent to the third-party and duplicates are sent to the customer.

142. D.

The expiration date for equity options is the Saturday after the third Friday of the month in which the options are scheduled to expire.

143. A.

Development wells involve existing oil wells that are in production. These programs carry a lower degree of risk than exploratory well programs therefore they will have a lower expected return.

144. B.

The rights of limited partners to inspect the books and records of the limited partnership are a part of the Uniform Limited Partnership Act and need not be written into the limited partnership agreement.

145. A.

Any changes in holdings by the corporate officer must be reported immediately to the officer's company.

146. C.

Each of the choices is an exempt security except for private placements, which are exempt transactions.

147. C.

A registered representative may only provide a copy of the preliminary prospectus during the 20-day cooling off period.

148. D.

Choices A, B, and C are all considered manipulative, since they involve trades designed to make the public believe that the trading volume is higher than it actually is.

149. C.

The hypothecation of customer securities to finance a debit balance is permitted under the Securities Act of 1933.

150. D.

All of these functions are performed by the investment banker.

151. D.

The total volume for the last four weeks was 135,000 shares (30,000 + 40,000 + 35,000 + 30,000) for an average weekly volume of 33,750 against 1% of the shares outstanding, which is 40,000 shares. The company president may sell 40,000 shares, which is the greater of 1% of the shares outstanding or the 4-week average weekly volume under the restrictions.

152. C.

Shares purchased in a Regulation D offering are deemed restricted securities that must be sold under Rule 144 unless they have been held fully paid for two years by a non-affiliated person.

153. B.

Reallowance, selling group concession, underwriter's concession and spread is the order from smallest to largest.

154. B.

Because the order is a round lot order to sell at the close it will receive a price close to the closing price.

155. C.

A redemption notice is used to call all or part of an outstanding bond issue.

156. A.

Orders cannot be accepted with the red herring or tombstone ad placed during the 20-day cooling off period.

157. A.

The order is a buy stop limit order that is triggered at or above 55. Since the first trade is at 55 the order becomes a limit order to buy at 55 (or better). It may be filled on the second trade at 55.

158. A.

On the ex-dividend date, the specialist will reduce buy limits and sell stops, which are the orders entered below current market prices.

159. C.

The FINRA 5% Mark-up Policy addresses sales concession charged on a security transaction when a member acts as a dealer or principal.

160. D.

Tombstone ads are not an offer to buy or sell securities.

161. B.

This is a violation of FINRA rules. Representatives are not permitted to guarantee against customer losses.

162. D.

A put option is in-the-money when the market price is below than the strike price. When the market price is less than 30, the long put will be in-the-money.

163. C.

A short straddle position is looking for the profit from selling a call and a put with the same expiration date and strike price of the same underlying security; this strategy works best in a neutral or sideways market.

164. A.

A hot issue is a securities offering to the public that immediately trades above the public offering price in the secondary market.

165. C.

Intrinsic value, simply, is the amount that an option is in-the-money. A call is in-the-money when the market price of the underlying security is above the strike price; a put is in-the-money when the market price of the underlying security is below the strike price, regardless of whether the call or put is bought (held) or sold (written). Choice A refers to the options time value, which is the premium portion of the intrinsic value (intrinsic value minus premium = time value).

166. A.

Exploratory oil and gas wells are ones that are drilled in unproven fields, typically away from a producing development well.

167. A.

Limited liquidity, interests in a non-registered limited partnership make the shares highly illiquid and difficult to find a market. IRS scrutiny of non-registered limited partnerships is also a negative aspect of these arrangements.

168. A.

The offering may not exceed $5,000,000. Securities offered via Regulation A are considered exempt securities not registered with the SEC although an offering statement must be filed with the SEC.

169. C.

The 200,000 shares of repurchased stock (treasury stock) are a secondary offering. The new shares are a primary offering. Since this offering includes both a primary distribution and a secondary distribution, it is called a split offering.

170. A.

The red herring prospectus may be sent to customers during the cooling-off period.

171. C.

Once a firm agrees to participate in an underwriting, it may no longer purchase that security for its own account, so it must stop making a market in that security (II). Stabilization is only allowed in connection with a new issue, so it could happen as part of the new issue (III), but not otherwise. Stabilization is the support of the price so the new shares can be sold to the public.

172. D.

All of the above would be considered.

173. C.

Securities sold for the first time to the public are done so through an initial public offering, which would be the primary offering of these securities.

174. C.

The broker/dealer is permitted to contact other firms that expressed an interest in the last 60 days. Customers that expressed an unsolicited interest may be contact, provided that such interest took place within the last 10, not 60 days.

175. A.

Time and demand deposits are the banking activities of commercial retail banks, not investment banks.

176. C.

The spread is the sum of the management fee and the underwriters' concession.

177. A.

An immediate-or-cancel order is an immediate market execution that may result in a partial fill. Remaining shares not filled will be canceled.

178. D.

The tombstone ad only provides information about a securities offering; it is not an offer to buy or sell shares.

179. A.

Sell stop orders are entered below the current market price not above or at.

180. B.

An odd lot order (an order for less than 100 shares) to buy "at the close" is executed after the close of the market at the closing asked price of the day. There may be an odd lot differential charged.

181. A.

The buy limit order would be reduced by $0.55, to $39.45.

182. D.

Time and price discretion are assumed for trades made on the behalf of customers.

183. A.

Duplicate confirmations and statements are provided upon request.

184. B.

SEC Rule 17a-4 (Books and Records) requires I and II to be maintained.

185. A.

The position is an income combination where the customer expects the price of ADM to rise. Since the premium received is the gain (less the difference between the strike price and market price of ADM), the break even for this position is $22 ($30 - $8 = $22).

186. C.

Stock splits and stock dividends will increase the number of shares while decreasing the exercise price.

187. D.

A registered representative in violation of FINRA's Rules of Fair Practice may be subject to censure, fine, suspension, or expulsion.

188. C.

It would be difficult for a limited partnership to avoid the centralization of management since the business needs to have someone in control of its operations and make business decisions on behalf of the partnership.

189. C.

Democracy provisions in a limited partnership agreement allow limited partners some say in the matters of the partnership except the transferability of property or repurchase plans.

190. C.

Selling and offering costs are deducted from the proceeds of a DPP offering while the acquisition and organizational costs are net the proceeds received by the DPP.

191. D.

An intrastate offering under Rule 147 must meet all of the listed choices.

192. D.

All of these must be included in the registration statement.

193. D.

Promotional materials may be sent to customers as long as it is accompanied with the prospectus.

194. A.

The securities of a customer held by a securities firm must be segregated from the firm's securities.

195. C.

A husband and wife would be counted as a single investor regardless of how they hold title. A person with a net worth of $1,000,000 is considered an accredited investor. An investor with a net worth of $250,000 would be considered a non-accredited investor. All the members of an investment club formed to purchase the securities would be counted separately.

196. D.

Because the selling group is permitted to sell their allotment of shares back to the syndicate, they are not at risk in the offering.

197. A.

A non-affiliated person is not subject to the volume limitations of Rule 144 for securities owned at least two years on a fully paid basis.

198. B.

If the stock market is consolidating, it is trading in a very narrow range and the trendline will be sideways.

199. B.

A partial fill of 700 of the 1,000 shares took place, resulting in a reduction to 300 shares subject to being filled either at 38 or Stop 42.

200. D.

zr stands for a zero coupon bond.

201. C.

Investment Companies are regulated by the Investment Company Act of 1940, as well as Section 2(a)1 of the Securities Act of 1933.

202. A.

The sell stop order would be triggered by the first trade at or below the stop price. The trade at 37 would therefore trigger the order. When a stop order is triggered, it becomes a market order, which would require an immediate execution at the best available price, which would occur on the next trade @ 36.75.

203. C.

An all-or-none order is an order to buy multiple round lots at a set price when the customer is willing to wait for full execution at the chosen price.

204. D.

The ticks are reduced by $0.70. If the stock opens at $29.30, that trade is considered a zero plus tick, which is the lowest price at which the stock may be sold short.

205. C.

Confirm must take place periodically regarding the continuance of the limited power of attorney and checks may never be issued in the representative's name.

206. A.

Stocks begin trading ex-dividend two business days prior to the record date. Since the ex-dividend date was Monday, July 8, the record date was Wednesday, July 10. Common stocks settle T+3 in a regular-way settlement. To be entitled to a dividend, the client must be on the record books on July 10 settling on Friday, July 5. Remember a cash settlement is same day, so Wednesday, July 10 is also an option.

207. A.

Arbitration is generally less costly than litigation.

208. B.

Uncovered call writing is the most speculative position.

209. A.

The customer received $800 in premiums through the sale of the call and the put in this short straddle. Upon exercise of the put, the customer was under an obligation to purchase DEF stock at $40 per share from the holder of the put (indicating a declining market) and since the customer was only able to sell the stock for $35, experienced a net loss of $500 on the stock transaction. The $800 gain in premiums less the $500 loss equals a net profit of $300.

210. C.

In a bankruptcy proceeding for a limited partnership the order of liquidation (which is similar to that of a corporation) is secured creditors, unsecured creditors, limited partners (to the extent of their pro-rata shares), and the general partner.

211. D.

All of these statements describe the responsibilities of the management in a real estate limited partnership.

212. C.

Intangible drilling costs are the primary deduction available in an oil and gas drilling partnership in the first year.

213. B.

The 1933 Act governs stock and bond offerings of corporations. Municipal bonds are considered exempt from registration while railroad stocks are issuance of common carriers that must register with the Interstate Commerce Commission.

214. A.

The time between the filing of the registration statement and its effective date is the cooling-off period, which typically lasts 20 days.

215. C.

A dealer must send customers in the secondary market a prospectus within 90 days after an initial public offering or within 40 days after a secondary or subsequent primary offering.

216. B.

A customer account with a free credit balance is required to receive account statements at least quarterly.

217. C.

Regulation D offerings are private placements.

218. C.

Rule 506 and Rule 505 offerings permit up to 35 non-accredited investors and an unlimited number of accredited investors.

219. B.

The spouse of an affiliated person would also be considered an affiliated person subject to volume restrictions.

220. C.

An All-or-None underwriting would be canceled if all of the offering cannot be sold.

221. B.

A specialist is permitted to accept a good-till-canceled (GTC) order.

222. A.

cv stands for a convertible bond.

223. D.

This is an Eastern Account or undivided account underwriting. Even though the dealer sold their allotment, they would be liable for 10% of the unsold allotment or $300,000.

224. D.

The order is a stop limit order. It is triggered at or below the stop price. When the order is triggered it turns into a limit order.

225. C.

The DOT system is subject to size limitations.

226. B.

FINRA firms may not transact securities business with non-FINRA members.

227. D.

Customers do not have access to the firm's income statement.

228. D.

All of the following are acceptable situations for a firm to collect fees.

229. D.

All of these activities require the prior written approval by a registered principal of a firm.

230. D.

100% of the premium must be deposited for the purchase of an option.

231. D.

8,000 is the limit on the number of contracts that are permitted to be held on the same side of the market in the same underlying security in order to prevent manipulation of the security's market price.

232. A.

A spread is the difference in strike prices (price spread) or time (time spread) relative to the purchase and sale of calls or puts on the same underlying security.

233. B.

Because the put option on XYZ expired worthless, the customer is out the $400 paid in premiums. As for the stock position, $1,000 gain was made, resulting in a net profit of $1,000 - $400 = $600.

234. B.

The initial position was an opening purchase; to close out, the customer would need to enter a closing sale.

235. C.

The purpose of purchasing the put is to protect the customer against a downside risk that the stock will lose market value. Holding the put allows the holder to "put" the stock to the writer at the strike price, which presumably will be lower than the exercise price.

236. D.

The cost of the stock would be $55 + $4 for the call premium, resulting in an adjusted cost basis of $59 per share.

237. D.

Option writers benefit the most when the market price of an underlying security remains the same as the strike price of the associated option.

238. A.

The customer bought an option, paying a $10 premium and at the same time sold an option for which they received a $4 premium for a $6 loss. If the calls expire worthless, a net loss of $600 would be realized.

239. C.

As interest rates rise, debt security prices fall. In anticipation of buying puts or selling calls would be the appropriate strategy.

240. D.

An uncovered call is the riskiest option position. Presumably if the writer were exercised against, they would need to go into the market to purchase the shares. The market price theoretically can grow on an unlimited basis.

241. A.

Income from rents would be the first revenue source for the public housing revenue bonds.

242. B.

To close out the position, the customer would need make a closing purchase of the same options contract. This would result in $4,750 received less $2,125 paid = $2,625 net profit (before taxes).

243. B.

The multiplier for options of the NYSE index is 100, therefore the holder would be entitled to receive $700 in cash ($87 - $80 × $100 = $700).

244. D.

Each of the choices listed are disadvantages associated with a limited partnership direct participation program.

245. B.

The depletion allowance for oil and gas limited partnerships is an advantage that is similar to depreciation in real estate.

246. C.

Investors in a partnership do not have control over management.

247. C.

Profit is not a corporate characteristic considered by the IRS toward limited partnerships.

248. C.

The flow through of tax consequences to limited partners and limited liability to the shareholders are distinct advantages of these programs.

249. D.

All of the choices should be used to evaluate a direct participation program.

250. C.

The writer of the 10 calls received a total of $4,750 for the sale. If the price of the stock moves above $40, as long as it goes no higher than the strike price ($40) plus the premium received ($4.75), setting the break even at $44.75 per share.

PRACTICE TEST #2

1. Which option contract would be out-of-the-money?

I.	A call with a strike price of $20 with the underlying security priced at $18
II.	A call with a strike price of $20 with the underlying security priced at $22
III.	A put with a strike price of $30 with the underlying security priced at $35
IV.	A put with a strike price of $30 with the underlying security priced at $25

    A.   I and IV

    B.   I and III

    C.   II and IV

    D.   II and III

2. A customer purchased an ABC 8% bond on Tuesday, March 20th. The payment dates on the bond are January 1 and July 1. How much accrued interest will the customer have to pay?

    A. $16.67

    B. $16.89

    C. $18.22

    D. $18.44

3. A company is set to elect two members of its board of directors. A customer with 600 shares of the company stock wishes to vote for one officer. Which of the following would be true?

I.	The customer should vote using the statutory method
II.	The customer should vote using the cumulative method
III.	Under each method the customer has a total of 1200 votes to cast
IV.	Under each method the customer has a total of 600 votes to cast

    A.   I and III

    B.   I and IV

    C.   II and III

    D.   II and IV

4. A customer purchases 1 MNO 70 Call @ $4 and 1 MNO 70 Put @ $2 with MNO trading at $62. If MNO moves to $81, what is the profit/loss (assuming exercise of the call)?

    A. $500 profit

    B. $500 loss

    C. $600 profit

    D. $600 loss

5. A customer is looking to buy a security so that in five years she will be able to purchase shares of a corporation based on a subscription price. Which of the following statements are true?

> I. The customer is buying a right
>
> II. The customer is buying a warrant
>
> III. The subscription price will be lower than the market price
>
> IV. The subscription price will be above the market price

A. I and III

B. II and III

C. I and IV

D. II and IV

6. A customer purchases 1 XYZ 40 Call @ $6 and sells 1 XYZ 30 Call @ $3 in a cash account. The price of XYZ stock is trading at $35. What is the break-even point for this position?

A. $34

B. $38

C. $43

D. $47

7. A customer purchases a municipal bond at 97 in secondary trading, with the bond maturing in ten years. The customer sells the bond after five years for 103. What is the customer's gain or loss on sale?

A. No gain or loss

B. $30 gain

C. $45 gain

D. $60 gain

8. A customer sells 1 ABC $30 Call @ $3 and 1 ABC 30 Put @ $5 with the price of ABC trading at $25. The maximum gain for this position is:

A. $300

B. $400

C. $600

D. $800

9. A customer with $10,000 to invest in a government security, wants to buy at a discount with a maturity in three months. Which government security should the investor purchase?

A. Treasury bills

B. Treasury notes

C. Treasury bonds

D. Treasury receipts

10. A mature company that is in a stable industry, paying high dividends, has what type of stock?

A. Growth

B. Cyclical

C. Income

D. Speculative

11. A put writer sold a 35 XYZ put for $225 with no position in the underlying stock. What would be the maximum loss for this option position?

A. $3,275

B. Unlimited

C. $3,500

D. $225

12. A security is registered in the name of A. Jones and Mrs. B. Jones. Which of the following is correct regarding the endorsement of certificates?

A. The certificates can be endorsed by A. Jones only

B. The certificates can be endorsed by A. Jones and Mrs. Jones

C. The certificates can be endorsed by Mrs. B. Jones only

D. The certificates can be endorsed by A. Jones and Mrs. B. Jones

13. All of the following are authorities of the MSRB EXCEPT:

A. Rule-making

B. Self-regulation

C. Market transparency

D. Enforcement

14. An individual investor looking to receive a pro rata share of company dividends and the ability to vote for members of the board of directors should purchase what type of stock?

    A. Common stock

    B. Preferred stock

    C. Prior preferred stock

    D. Convertible preferred stock

15. An investor purchasing a bond with no pledge of specific collateral that is backed by the full faith and credit of the issuer has purchased what type of bond?

    A. Equipment trust certificate

    B. Mortgage bond

    C. Debenture

    D. Income bond

16. Given the end-of-day price Thursday, August 15, an investor who purchased 300 shares of Investors Fund on the morning of Thursday, August 15, would have paid a total of:

Fund Name Change	NAV	POP	Net Asset Change
Investors Fund	$5.60	$6.03	+0.02
Wealth Fund	$7.80	$8.50	+0.01

    A. $1,680

    B. $1,680 plus sales charge

    C. $1,809

    D. $1,809 plus sales charge

17. GNMA securities are guaranteed by the full faith and credit of the U.S. Government, which ensures:

    A. Payment of the principal only

    B. Payment of the principal, interest, and late payment

    C. Timely payment of principal only

    D. Timely payment of principal and interest

18. If a customer has an account that has a credit balance, how frequently must statements of account be sent?

    A. Monthly

    B. Quarterly

    C. Semi-annually

    D. Annually

19. In a customer's account, the opening transaction is the purchase of $10,000 ABC convertible bonds at par. Under Regulation T, how much cash must be deposited?

    A. $2,000

    B. $2,500

    C. $5,000

    D. $10,000

20. In the OTC market, what is the difference between a market maker's bid and ask prices referred to as?

    A. Spread

    B. Mark-up

    C. Mark-down

    D. Commission

21. Mrs. Jackson wants to purchase a variety of municipal securities for her portfolio and wants to spread out her risk. Which of the following is the least important in this diversification?

    A. Location of the issuer

    B. The maturity of the bonds issued

    C. Quality of the bonds

    D. The issue's denomination

22. A 10% Par Convertible Bond is issued convertible at $50/share when the parity price of the bond is $975. What is the parity price of the stock?

    A. $19.50

    B. $48.75

    C. $49.36

    D. $50.00

23. The funds accumulated in a sinking fund may be used for all of the following EXCEPT:

A. To redeem the bonds at maturity

B. To exercise a partial call

C. To pay a dividend to bondholders

D. To repurchase bonds in open market

24. Use the following information to determine how many shares of ABC traded:

XZY	ABC	GGGSLD	DEA
8.25	3s30	10.000s25	3s35

A. 3,000

B. 300

C. 30

D. 3

25. What agency/organization makes mortgage loans to farmers?

A. Federal Farm Credit Consolidated System-wide Banks

B. Federal Land Bank Associations

C. Credit associations

D. The Banks for Cooperatives

26. To what does the Trust Indenture Act of 1939 apply?

A. Corporate bond offerings in a single state

B. Multi-state corporate bond offering

C. U.S. Government Securities

D. Multi-state common stock offering

27. What is the difference between an open-end investment company and a closed-end investment company?

A. Investment objective

B. Fund management

C. Fund capitalization

D. Method used to calculate net asset value (NAV)

28. What is the most important suitability consideration for a client who chooses to purchase a variable annuity?

A. Monthly payments will remain fixed

B. There will be a penalty for the early withdrawal of funds

C. Assumed interest rate (AIR) will vary

D. Benefit payments will vary

29. What risk is associated with a security that may lose value due to a drop in stock prices?

A. Credit risk

B. Market risk

C. Capital risk

D. Call risk

30. What would be involved in a transaction in which a shareholder sells his shares to another investor?

A. The issuing corporation

B. The rights agent and agent of the shareholder

C. The shareholder and the new investor

D. The transfer agent and the registrar

31. Which of the following best describes a Keogh plan?

I.	Tax-deferred investment
II.	Retirement account
III.	Tax-free trust

A. I only

B. I and II

C. II and III

D. I, II, and III

32. Which of the following circumstances would allow the management of a mutual fund to change the investment objectives of the fund?

   A. The shareholders have been given 30 days' prior notification

   B. The shareholders have been given the right to switch funds at no expense with objectives similar to those that the fund presently has

   C. The fund's NAV has declined by more than 50% of the original offering price

   D. 50% of the fund's shareholders holding the outstanding voting securities have given authorization

33. Which of the following is not a characteristic of preferred stock?

   A. Company ownership

   B. A fixed and guaranteed rate of return

   C. Perpetuity

   D. Priority over common stock for dividends

34. Which of the following is true for a mutual fund that charges a 12b-1 distribution fee?

   A. It is a no-load fund

   B. It is a loaded fund

   C. The distribution fee is charged to all shareholders of the fund

   D. The fund is always sold through broker/dealers only

35. Which of the following penalties may be assessed by the FINRA under the Summary Complaint Procedure?

I.	Censure
II.	A fine of $2,500
III.	A fine of any amount
IV.	Expulsion

   A. I only

   B. I and II

   C. I, II, and III

   D. I, II, III, and IV

36. Which of the following statements are correct regarding the relationship between the yields of the Bond Buyers 20 Bond Index and the Bond Buyer 11 Bond Index?

   A. The yield on the 11 Bond Index would be lower than the yield on the 20 Bond Index

   B. The yield on the 11 Bond Index would be the same as the yield on the 20 Bond Index

   C. The yield on the 11 Bond Index would be higher than the yield on the 20 Bond Index

   D. There is no relationship between the yield of the 11 Bond Index and the yield of the 20 Bond Index

37. Which of the following terms are paired when liquidating open-end investment company shares that have a sales charge?

   A. Ask price; sales price

   B. Sales price; NAV

   C. NAV; sales redemption price

   D. Bid price; public offering price

38. Which of the following would be possible disadvantages of an equipment leasing program?

I.	The potential for the lessee to default on the payments
II.	The recapture of tax credits
III.	Investors may realize a reportable income for tax purposes in excess of realized cash flow
IV.	A low residual value at the end of the lease term

   A. I and II

   B. II and IV

   C. I, II, and III

   D. I, II, III, and IV

39. Which of the following would take place if a customer enters an order to purchase 300 shares of ACME Mfg at $20 per share, was informed that the shares were purchased at $19, and later discovered that the trade was executed at $20?

A. The registered representative would be required to make up the difference

B. The floor broker would be required to make up the difference if it was the mistake was from the floor broker

C. The broker/dealer would be required to make up the difference

D. The customer would be required to pay $20 per share for ACME Mfg

40. Which system is used by broker/dealers trading OTC stocks that are not listed on the NASDAQ?

A. Green sheets

B. Blue sheets

C. Pink sheets

D. Yellow sheets

41. A company has convertible bonds outstanding that have a conversion price of $25. If there is an anti-dilution clause in the trust indenture, what would be the effect of a 10% stock dividend?

A. Bondholders would receive a check for $50

B. Bondholders would receive four shares of the common stock

C. The conversion price would be reduced to $22.72

D. There would be no effect

42. A customer (with no securities positions) sells 1 ABC September 30 put for a premium of $3, when the price of ABC stock is $30 per share. If the writer is assigned an exercise notice when the stock falls to $25 per share, what is the profit or loss?

A. $100 profit

B. $100 loss

C. $200 profit

D. $200 loss

43. A customer makes an initial transaction in a margin account of 100 shares of ABC @ $50 a share. Under Reg. T requirements, what is the customer's initial equity?

A. $1,000

B. $1,500

C. $2,500

D. $5,000

44. A customer purchases 1 JKL 75 Put @ $4 and sells 1 JKL 85 Put @ $8 in a cash account with the price of JKL trading at $77. What is the maximum gain for this position?

A. $200

B. $400

C. $600

D. $800

45. UGMA stands for:

A. Uniform Grant to Minors Act

B. Uniform Grant to Minorities Act

C. Uniform Gift to Minors Act

D. Uniform Gift to Minorities Act

46. Each of the following is a type of municipal note EXCEPT:

A. AONs

B. BANs

C. PNs

D. RANs

47. A customer receiving interest income from holding a qualified private activity bond would pay which of the following taxes?

A. Ordinary income

B. Alternative minimum tax

C. Capital gains tax

D. Excise taxes

48. A customer sells 1 ABC July 40 call for $5 per share and buys 1 ABC November 40 call for $8 per share. Closing transactions are executed prior to expiration with the purchase of 1 ABC July 40 call for $2 per share and sale of 1 ABC November 40 call for $6 per share. What is the profit/loss?

A. $100 profit

B. $100 loss

C. $300 profit

D. $300 loss

49. A firm may do all of the following regarding customer statements EXCEPT:

A. Hold the statements for two months if the customer is traveling within the U.S.

B. Hold the statements for 90 days while the customer is traveling outside the U.S.

C. Forward the statements to a P.O. Box of the customer

D. Forward the customer's statements to the home of the registered representative

50. A municipal securities representative may do all of the following during his apprenticeship period EXCEPT:

A. Complete the municipal securities representative examination

B. Make contact with the firm's research department regarding questions about the municipal securities market

C. Provide advice to municipal securities issuers

D. Make a purchase of municipal securities for own account

51. A registered representative looking to send a letter to customers regarding stocks the customers own or are contemplating buying may not use which of the following language?

A. A 4 to 5 point gain in the stock should be used to invest in another fast moving situation

B. The new stock being recommended will absolutely go up 5 or 6 points if you buy it now

C. You should buy the stock now before the institutions get into it; I will mail you a research report immediately

D. Each of these statements may be deemed improper

52. A stock's tangible net asset value per share is the same as:

A. Book value

B. Market value

C. Par value

D. Stated value

53. All of the following statements concerning variable annuities are correct EXCEPT:

A. Variable annuities provide professional management of a portfolio

B. A variable annuity portfolio protects against capital loss

C. A variable annuity portfolio may consist of shares in other mutual funds

D. A variable annuity holder may vote to change investment objectives

54. An investment in an individual retirement plan may be done by which of the following?

I. A self-employed individual with a Keogh plant

II. A corporate employee that is covered by a company pension with a second job not covered

III. A corporate employee not covered by a pension or profit-sharing plan

A. I only

B. III only

C. II and III

D. I, II and III

55. CMOs were designed in recognition of the disadvantages of GNMAs by:

A. Having a longer than expected average life

B. Receiving more favorable tax treatment

C. Providing better guarantee

D. Providing a steadier cash flow

56. Given the end of day price Thursday, August 15, the first page of the prospectus of Wealth Fund would indicate that the sales charge for a small purchase of the fund is what percentage of the offering price?

Fund Name Change	NAV	POP	Net Asset Change
Investors Fund	$5.60	$6.03	+0.02
Wealth Fund	$7.80	$8.50	+0.01

A. 1.00%

B. 8.20%

C. 8.50%

D. 9.00%

57. How are customer securities valued in a liquidation under SIPC?

A. By their current market value at the date of distribution

B. By the customers' original cost basis

C. By their current market value at the time of liquidation

D. By the lower of the customers' cost basis or fair market value

58. If Investor A wishes to purchase a bond from Investor B, to whom is accrued interest paid?

A. Investor A

B. Investor B

C. The securities firm selling the bonds

D. B and C

59. In January, a customer purchases 1 GCS July 40 put for $5, with the price of GCS stock at 40. The maximum loss the customer could sustain by the expiration date is:

A. $500

B. $3,500

C. $4,000

D. An unlimited amount

60. In their advertisements, XYZ Brokerage uses a ranking of growth mutual funds that was produced by a national, independent publication, based on total return. What would FINRA require in the ads?

I.	The rankings may not be based on returns that are less than one year old
II.	The ranking must be based on the returns from the most recent calendar year
III.	Rankings for periods of one, five, and ten-years must be shown
IV.	Headlines may not imply or state that a company is the best performer in the growth category

A. I and III

B. II and IV

C. I, II and III

D. I, II, III, and IV

61. Options are available for which of the following types of securities?

I.	Government securities
II.	Foreign currencies
III.	Stock indices
IV.	Exchange-traded funds

A. I and III

B. II and IV

C. I, II, and IV

D. I, II, III, and IV

62. The bond counsel performs a review of which of the following when issuing an unqualified opinion?

A. Any judicial edicts

B. The state constitution or municipal charter

C. State and Federal tax law

D. A, B, and C

63. The purchase of an Apr 20 ABC put and an Apr 20 ABC call is known as a:

A. Short straddle

B. Long straddle

C. Vertical spread

D. Option spread

64. Use the following information for the question below.

XZY	ABC	GGGSLD	DEA
8.25	3s30	10.000s25	3s35

Which of the following statements are correct regarding XZY stock?

I.	500 shares traded at 8.25
II.	100 shares traded at 8.25
III.	100 shares traded at 8

A. I only

B. II only

C. III only

D. II and III

65. What amount of capital may be raised through a Rule 505 offering?

A. $500,000

B. $1,500,000

C. $5,000,000

D. Unlimited

66. What form of compensation does an investment adviser managing clients' funds receive?

A. Fees

B. Commissions

C. Either A or B

D. Both A and B

67. What is the largest monthly payment to the holder of a variable annuity that will occur under the following pay out options?

A. Life annuity payment

B. Life annuity period certain payment

C. Joint life annuity payment

D. Unit refund life annuity payment

68. What is the name of the exchange floor dealer who is responsible for maintaining a fair and orderly market and managing a book of unexecuted stop and limit orders?

A. Market maker

B. Floor broker

C. Specialist

D. Floor trader

69. What risk is associated with investment grade bonds?

A. Credit risk

B. Selection risk

C. Inflationary risk

D. Timing risk

70. What would be used when analyzing the sources of revenue and expenses in a limited partnership?

A. An analysis of capital

B. An analysis of cash flow

C. An analysis of liquidity

D. An analysis of the portfolio

71. Which of the following best describes a restricted long account?

    A. Above 50% initial margin requirements; below 25% maintenance level

    B. Above 50% initial margin requirements; below 30% maintenance level

    C. Below 50% initial margin; above the 25% maintenance level

    D. Below 50% initial margin requirements; above the 30% maintenance level

72. Which of the following investments would best be used as a hedge against inflation?

    A. Corporate bonds

    B. Series EE bonds

    C. Variable annuities

    D. Face amount certificates

73. Which of the following is NOT a recordkeeping requirement for broker-dealers?

    A. Maintenance of a written-complaint file

    B. Maintenance of a record of broker errors

    C. Maintenance of net capital and minimum net capital requirements

    D. Maintenance of a record of positions held and trades executed for each customer

74. Which of the following is true of a transaction involving the purchase of foreign securities?

    | I. | The customer will need to purchase American Depository Receipts (ADRs) |
    | II. | The customer will purchase the shares from the issuing foreign corporation |
    | III. | Resale of the shares may be difficult if not registered with the SEC |

    A. I and II

    B. I only

    C. I and III

    D. I, II, and III

75. Which of the following persons would not be registered?

    A. A person soliciting business for a firm's investment banking activities

    B. A person whose duties are strictly clerical in nature

    C. A person who provides advice regarding municipal securities

    D. A person soliciting orders from customers on behalf of a registered representative

76. Which of the following statements are correct regarding U.S. Government agency securities?

    | I. | These securities are a direct obligation of the U.S. Government |
    | II. | Agency debt has higher yields than other securities that are issued by the U.S. Government |
    | III. | FNMA is publicly traded |
    | IV. | GNMA trades on the New York Stock Exchange |

    A. II and III

    B. I and III

    C. II and IV

    D. I, II, III, and IV

77. Which of the following transactions may NOT be done in a cash account?

    A. Buying stock

    B. Short stock sales

    C. Mutual fund purchases

    D. Buying options

78. Which of the following would NOT be considered a discretionary transaction?

A. A customer wants to buy 500 shares of ACME when the registered representative decides

B. The customer wants to buy some shares of ACME; the registered representative determines when and how many shares

C. A customer wants to buy some shares of ACME at the opening, letting the registered representative determine how many shares

D. A customer wants to purchase 500 shares of growth stock and the registered representative buys 500 shares of ACME

79. Which one of the following statements is correct concerning American-style stock options?

A. An American stock option must be exercised prior to expiration

B. The seller of a put is obligated to purchase 100 shares of the underlying security at the market price

C. At expiration, a stock option will become a market order for the underlying security

D. The buyer of a put has a bearish outlook of the market

80. XYZ Securities has participated in an underwriting of common stock for General Conglomerate Corp (GCC). How must this information be disclosed to the public?

I.	On all GCC confirmations
II.	On all GCC research reports
III.	For a period of two years

A. I only

B. II only

C. I and II

D. I, II, and III

81. A company is calling the preferred stock it issued at 102. The preferred stock is convertible into 4 shares of common stock, which is trading at $20 per share. What should the holder of the preferred stock do?

A. Allow the preferred stock to be called by the company

B. Do nothing, as the company cannot force shareholders to sell the preferred stock

C. Convert the preferred stock into shares of common stock

D. File a complaint with the SEC

82. A customer (with no securities positions) sells 1 ABC September 30 put for a premium of $3, when the price of ABC stock is $30 per share. What would the stock price of ABC need to be just prior to expiration for the customer to break even?

A. $30

B. $27

C. $25

D. $20

83. Municipal bonds settle regular way in:

A. One day

B. Three days

C. Five days

D. Seven days

84. The sales load of a mutual fund is 8% and has a 1.5% underwriter's concession. If the net asset value is $16.50, the offering price is determined by dividing NAV by:

A. 91.5%

B. 92.0%

C. 108.0%

D. 115.0%

85. A customer purchases 1 MNO 70 Call @ $4 and 1 MNO 70 Put @ $2 with MNO trading at $62. What is the maximum loss?

A. $0

B. $300

C. $500

D. $600

86. Which of the following type of corporate securities is most senior?

A. Common stock

B. Preferred stock

C. Debenture

D. Mortgage bond

87. A customer sells 1 ABC $30 Call @ $3 and 1 ABC 30 Put @ $5 with the price of ABC trading at $25. If the price of ABC moves to $19 and the customer receives an exercise notice for the put, what is the profit/loss?

A. $800 profit

B. $300 profit

C. $300 loss

D. $800 loss

88. A customer sells 1 ABC July 40 call for $5 and buys 1 ABC November 40 call for $8. What is the break-even price?

A. $37

B. $40

C. $43

D. $48

89. A firm receives an order from a customer to purchase an over-the-counter security that is not listed on the NASDAQ system. To obtain the best price execution, which of the following would be required?

A. Contacting one market maker

B. Contacting two market makers

C. Contacting three market makers

D. Contacting every market maker

90. A municipality wishes to sell securities by a competitive bid underwriting. It will need to publish all of the following EXCEPT:

A. Whether the bonds are general obligation or revenue bonds

B. The registration provisions of the bonds

C. The amount of the good faith deposit

D. The names of the syndicate members

91. A registered representative sells a limited partnership to his customer, however the representative's firm has not approved the offering. This practice is known as:

A. Disintermediation

B. Selling away

C. Hypothecation

D. Front-running

92. A trade between two broker/dealers settles when?

A. Trade date (T+0)

B. Business day after the trade date (T+1)

C. Three business days after trade date (T+3)

D. Seven business days after trade date (T+7)

93. An employee of a member firm participating in the underwriting of a hot issue wishes to sell some of the shares to a spouse. This could be done if:

A. The amount of shares sold are deemed insubstantial

B. The shares purchased are in line with the normal investment practice of the spouse

C. Under no circumstances

D. A and B

94. An investor buys shares of an open-end mutual fund in January when the BID (NAV) is $14 and the ASK price is $15. The investor redeems the shares in August when the NAV is $19 and the ASK price is $20. What is the tax liability?

A. Long-term capital gain of $5 per share

B. Long-term capital gain of $6 per share

C. Short-term capital gain of $4 per share

D. Short-term capital gain of $5 per share

95. Debt securities sold by the Federal Home Loan Bank are appropriate for investors looking for all of the following EXCEPT:

A. A short-term discount note

B. Interest that is exempt from local income taxes

C. Securities backed by pools of mortgages

D. Securities that are issued in book entry form

96. General Corp has a 10% bond outstanding. A customer owns one bond purchased for $1,100. When the next interest payment date occurs, the customer will receive:

A. $55

B. $50

C. $110

D. $100

97. How frequently must an investment company issue financial statements to its shareholders?

A. Monthly

B. Quarterly

C. Semi-annually

D. Annually

98. If the market is moving sideways, an investor may increase her yield by:

I.	Purchasing calls
II.	Writing calls
III.	Purchasing puts
IV.	Writing puts

A. I and III

B. II and III

C. II and IV

D. I and IV

99. In January, a customer purchases 1 GCS July 40 put for $5, with the price of GCS stock at 40. What is the maximum profit the customer could make by the expiration date of the option?

A. $500

B. $3,500

C. $4,000

D. An unlimited amount

100. Limited partners have the right to do which of the following?

I.	Inspect the books and records of the limited partnership
II.	Seek legal redress against the general partner for damages if the general partner wrongfully implements the proceeds of the offering
III.	Set the compensation level that the general partner will receive
IV.	Receive tax benefits that result from the operation of the partnership project

A. I and II

B. I and III

C. II and III

D. III and IV

101. Prior preferred stock provides what benefits?

A. It is issued before the regular preferred

B. Liquidation priority over common and preferred stock

C. Share convertibility at $6 per share

D. Dividends priority over common and preferred stock

102. The bond counsel renders an unqualified opinion on which of the following?

> I. The tax status of the bonds
> II. Treasury arbitrage regulations
> III. Reoffering yields
> IV. The validity of the issue

- A. I, II, and III
- B. II, III, and IV
- C. I, III, and IV
- D. I, II, and IV

103. A customer purchases 1 JKL 75 Put @ $4 and sells 1 JKL 85 Put @ $8 in a cash account with the price of JKL trading at $77. What is the maximum loss?

- A. $200
- B. $400
- C. $600
- D. $800

104. Use the following information for the question below:

XZY	ABC	GGGSLD	DEA
8.25	3s30	10.000s25	3s35

How many shares of DEA traded?

- A. 300
- B. 30
- C. 3
- D. 15

105. What are the initial minimum margin requirements under Regulation T and NYSE minimum maintenance requirements for long accounts?

- A. 25% / 30%
- B. 50% / 25%
- C. 50% / 30%
- D. 50% / 50%

106. What is an investment company that has no management fee and a relatively low percentage sales charge invested in a fixed portfolio of municipal or corporate bonds called?

- A. Closed-end investment company
- B. Open-end investment company
- C. Unit investment trust
- D. Face amount certificate company

107. What is the largest operating expense in a money market fund?

- A. Custodial fee
- B. Fee for auditing services
- C. Registration fees and taxes
- D. Management fees and advisory fees

108. What is the purpose of an illustration of rates of return in variable life insurance sales literature?

- A. To give customers a prediction of investment results under various scenarios
- B. To give customers a comparison of variable life insurance to other investment alternatives
- C. To show customers how the performance in the investment account may affect death benefits and cash values
- D. To illustrate to customers what payments should be expected

109. With what rules must a broker who extends credit for the purpose of purchasing or carrying margin stocks comply?

- A. Regulation G
- B. Regulation T
- C. Regulation U
- D. Regulation X

110. When an investor purchases a municipal bond at a premium, the book value of the bond is decreased during the bond's holding period. This accounting process is known as:

    A.   Depreciation of capital

    B.   Amortization of capital

    C.   Accretion of discount

    D.   Accrual of interest

111. Which of the following bonds will have the greatest change in price when interest rates increase from 8% to 10%?

    A.   An 8% bond maturing in two years

    B.   An 8% bond maturing in five years

    C.   An 8% bond maturing in ten years

    D.   An 8% bond maturing in seven years

112. A customer purchases a call with a strike price of $25 at a premium of $3. What is the break even for this option?

    A. $28

    B. $32

    C. $25

    D. $22

113. Which of the following is correct of an individual that is an active participant in an employer-sponsored qualified retirement plan?

    A.   Contributions to an IRA are not allowed

    B.   Contributions to an IRA are allowed, but do not grow tax deferred

    C.   Contributions to an IRA are allowed, but cannot be deducted from gross income

    D.   Contributions to an IRA would be allowed and can be deducted from gross income

114. Which of the following is not a risk to an owner of a GNMA security?

    A.   Fluctuation of principal as interest rates change

    B.   Reinvestment of principal and interest payments

    C.   Default by payers of interest and principal

    D.   Early return of investment

115. Which of the following is (are) correct regarding NASDAQ Level I?

I.	The highest bid price is shown
II.	The lowest asked price is shown
III.	Market makers in a listed security is shown
IV.	It permit market makers to change their quotes

    A.   I only

    B.   I and II

    C.   III and IV

    D.   I, II, III, and IV

116. Which of the following projects would not be financed with a revenue bond?

    A.   A bond issue to financing a toll bridge

    B.   A bond issue financing a sewerage system

    C.   A bond issue financing the construction of a school

    D.   A bond issue financing a power plant

117. Which of the following statements is correct concerning a registered representative that wishes to prepare and distribute a research report to customers?

I.	The report must be approved by a principal of the firm prior to distribution
II.	The report must be approved by a supervisory analyst prior to distribution
III.	The report must be approved by the NYSE prior to distribution
IV.	The report must be approved by the SEC prior to distribution

    A.   I only

    B.   I and II

    C.   III and IV

    D.   I, II, III, and IV

118. Which of the following would NOT be considered when determining a commission or mark-up?

    A. The firm's business expenses

    B. The type of security sold

    C. The trade size

    D. The security's availability

119. Which security has no fixed maturity date?

    A. Debenture

    B. Preferred stock

    C. Municipal bond

    D. Treasury bill

120. A company is involved in a rights offering with a subscription price of $43 per share, where the company's stock current market price is $45 per share. Three rights purchase one share of the company's common stock. The rights are currently trading at $0.75 per right. If the customer is not looking to own the company's stock, but desires to purchase some rights for speculative reasons, he should be advised that:

    A. The profit opportunity is immediate

    B. Market value of the shares must increase more for the investment to be profitable

    C. There is no profit opportunity available

    D. A rights offering is not an appropriate strategy for speculation

121. A customer gave a registered representative $15,000 with instructions to buy whatever stock "is best." The registered representative must:

    A. Follow the customer's verbal instructions

    B. Require the customer to give the verbal authorization to the representative's branch manager

    C. Accept the customer's verbal instructions if the registered representative is registered as an investment advisor

    D. Obtain written authorization from the customer prior to executing the instructions

122. A customer purchased an 8% bond with a yield to maturity of 9%. Several years later, the customer sells the bond to someone else. The yield to maturity on the bond is 7%. The customer has:

    A. A 2% loss

    B. A loss on the sale

    C. A gain on the sale

    D. No gain or loss

123. A customer purchases 1 JKL 75 Put @ $4 and sells 1 JKL 85 Put @ $8 in a cash account with the price of JKL trading at $77. Which of the following best describes this position's strategy?

I.	Bullish
II.	Bearish
III.	Credit
IV.	Debit

    A. I and III

    B. II and III

    C. II and IV

    D. I and IV

124. A customer purchases 1 XYZ 30 Call @ $6 and sells 1 XYZ 40 Call @ $3 in a cash account. The price of XYZ stock is trading at $35. What best describes the strategy of this position?

I.	Bullish
II.	Bearish
III.	Credit
IV.	Debit

    A. I and III

    B. II and III

    C. II and IV

    D. I and IV

125. A customer purchases a municipal bond at 105, with the bonds maturing five years later. What is the customer's gain or loss upon maturity?

A. No gain or loss

B. $50 gain

C. $500 loss

D. $500 gain

126. A customer sells 1 ABC $30 Call @ $3 and 1 ABC 30 Put @ $5 with the price of ABC trading at $25. If the price of ABC moves to $45 and the customer receives an exercise notice, what is her profit/loss?

A. $700 loss

B. $700 profit

C. $800 loss

D. $800 profit

127. A customer wishes to purchase a tax-free municipal bond. In which of the following should the customer invest?

A. General obligation bonds

B. Revenue bonds

C. Industrial revenue bonds

D. All of the above

128. A homeowner owns a home with an assessed valuation of $1,000,000 with a tax rate of 5 mills. The homeowner's tax liability would be:

A. $5

B. $50

C. $500

D. $5,000

129. A put purchased with a strike price of 30 has a premium of $3. What is the maximum profit?

A. $3,000

B. $30

C. $2,700

D. $27

130. A securities firm is asked for a quote on XYZ Corp stock. The firm provides a quote of $15 on the stock. The other firm asks to buy the stock at that price and is refused. What best describes the action of the firm holding XYZ Corp stock?

A. Interpositioning

B. Hypothecation

C. Disintermediation

D. Backing away

131. According to disclosure rules, a broker/dealer transacting a corporate securities trade must disclose to customers all of the following EXCEPT:

A. In what capacity the firm acted as in the transaction

B. Amount of commission being charged

C. Any interest rates on outstanding margin debit balances

D. If the customer bought or sold the security and at what price

132. An increase in the price of open-end investment shares from the initial purchase is:

A. Accretion

B. Amortization

C. Appreciation

D. Capital gain

133. An investor owns a security with a twenty-year maturity and interest coupons attached. What type of security does the investor own?

A. Treasury bills

B. Treasury notes

C. Treasury bonds

D. Treasury receipts

134. Each of the following penalties may be assessed by FINRA EXCEPT:

A. Expulsion

B. Imprisonment

C. Fines

D. Suspension

135. General Manufacturing Corp has a $6 preferred stock that is outstanding. Which of the following statements would be true?

A. Par value is $100 per share

B. There is no par value

C. The issue is considered prior preferred

D. The issue can be converted into common stock at $6 per share

136. How might a registered representative open a joint account with a public customer?

A. Only with the permission of the firm

B. If the registered representative participates only to the extent of their interest in the account

C. Both A and B

D. Under no circumstances

137. In a customer's account, the opening transaction is the purchase of $10,000 ABC convertible bonds at par. If the bonds appreciated to 110, what would be the SMA?

A. $50

B. $100

C. $500

D. $1,000

138. In order to create a limited partnership, which of the following must be filed with the state?

A. Limited partnership agreement

B. Limited partnership certificate

C. Subscription agreement

D. Underwriting agreement

139. Mr. Smith makes a purchase of municipal bonds from several different areas of the country. This strategy protects Mr. Smith from all of the following EXCEPT:

A. The impact of adverse legislation in one area

B. The economic decline in one area

C. An increase in interest rates

D. Default risk of one particular issuer

140. Recommendations by FINRA members must include which of the following disclosures?

I.	If the firm makes a market in the security
II.	The intention of a member to buy or sell the recommended security for its account
III.	If the member owns any right, warrants, or options in the recommended security
IV.	Whether the member participated in a public offering of any securities related to the recommended issue within the past three years

A. I and III

B. III and IV

C. I, II, and III

D. I, II, III, and IV

141. The fees that a firm charges for services must adhere to what standard?

A. Must be first approved by FINRA

B. Must represent a fair and reasonable charge

C. May not exceed 5%

D. Must be based on what the market can bear

142. The writer of a call with no position in the stock has a maximum profit that is_____and a loss potential that is_____.

A. Equal to the premium; unlimited

B. Unlimited; equal to the premium

C. Equal to the strike price plus the premium; unlimited

D. Unlimited; equal to the strike price minus the premium

143. Use the following information for the question below:

XZY	ABC	GGGSLD	DEA
8.25	3s30	10.000s25	3s35

Which of the following statements are correct regarding the GGG trade?

> I. 10,000 shares traded
>
> II. 10 shares traded
>
> III. The transaction was reported out of sequence
>
> IV. The shares were sold to the market maker

- A. I and III
- B. I and IV
- C. II and III
- D. II and IV

144. To what does the Instinet system relate?

- A. First market trading
- B. Second market trading
- C. Third market trading
- D. Fourth market trading

145. What is meant by "tax-exempt" municipal bonds?

- A. Interest is exempt from state and federal income tax
- B. Interest is exempt from state income tax
- C. Interest is exempt from federal income tax
- D. Capital gains are exempt from federal income tax

146. What is the margin requirement for a customer who bought $10,000 of a security and sold $10,000 of security on the same day?

- A. $5,000
- B. $10,000
- C. $20,000
- D. There is no margin requirement

147. What is the shortest maturity tranche of a CMO with three tranches?

- A. Receive principal only
- B. Receive interest only
- C. Receive interest and principal until it is retired
- D. Receive interest and principal after the second and third tranches receive interest and principal

148. What type of variable annuity pay out option would give a couple the opportunity to continue receiving income for the second individual upon the death of the first?

- A. Life annuity payments
- B. Life annuity period certain payments
- C. Life annuity rights of survivorship payments
- D. Joint life annuity payments

149. When may a firm sell a hot issue to its employee?

- A. When the firm is not an underwriter
- B. If the employee is not a registered representative
- C. Only if the hot issue is the stock of the firm
- D. Under no circumstances

150. Which of the following CANNOT authenticate a mutilated security?

- A. The issuer
- B. The registrar
- C. The transfer agent
- D. The broker/dealer

151. Which of the following is not a characteristic of high yield bonds?

- A. High volatility
- B. Purchased by fiduciaries
- C. High nominal interest rate
- D. Unsecured

152. Which of the following is the lowest investment grade bond rating?

A. AA

B. A

C. BBB

D. C

153. Which of the following occurs upon annuitization of a variable annuity contract?

A. The accumulation units value is used to determine the value of the annuity units

B. The accumulation units value is used to determine the number of annuity units

C. Separate account securities become taxable

D. Separate account securities are liquidated

154. Which of the following reasons are official statements provided for a municipal security new issue?

I. The issues that are larger than par value, MSRB requires issuance of an official statement

II. The SEC requires certain municipal issues to meet registration requirements

III. The dealers underwriting the issue require these documents for disclosure obligations to their retail customers

A. I only

B. III only

C. I and II

D. I, II, and III

155. Which of the following statements is true of a Rule 506 offering?

I. The offering is a negotiated transaction

II. An officer of the issuer may act as purchaser's representative

III. Non-accredited investors must meet certain minimum suitability standards

IV. A registered representative may act as a purchaser's representative

A. I, III, and IV

B. I and III

C. I only

D. I, II, III, and IV

156. Which of the following types of investment generates tax-deferred income?

A. Variable annuities

B. Open end mutual funds

C. Stocks

D. G.O. Bonds

157. Which of the following would not considered an investment company under the Investment Company Act of 1940?

A. A face amount certificate company

B. A unit investment trust company

C. A publicly-traded fund

D. A holding company

158. Which statement applies to warrants?

A. Warrants generally have voting rights

B. Warrants are the same as short-term options

C. Warrants cover 10 shares of the underlying stock

D. Warrants do not pay dividends

159. Trades made in the third market are required to be reported on the Consolidated Tape within what period of time?

A. 30 seconds

B. 60 seconds

C. 90 seconds

D. 120 seconds

160. Firm A is a member of the syndicate in a $1 million municipal bond underwriting with 20% participation in the offering. A total of $300,000 of the bonds remain unsold after the initial offering. Which of the following statements are correct?

I. Firm A would be liable for only $60,000 of the remaining bonds if it sold its entire allotment

II. Firm A would not be liable for the remaining bonds if it sold its entire allotted share

III. Firm A would be liable for only $60,000 of the remaining bonds if it sold none of its allotted share

IV. Firm A may be liable for more than $60,000 of the remaining bonds if it did not sell its allotment

A. I and III

B. I and IV

C. II and III

D. II and IV

161. A city and a school district exist as coterminous entities, both with outstanding bond issues and drawing from the same taxpayers for debt support. This would be an example of what type of debt?

A. Concentric

B. Contiguous

C. Direct

D. Overlapping

162. Who would execute an order from a member firm to buy 100 XYZ stock?

A. Registered representatives

B. Floor brokers

C. Specialists

D. Competitive traders

163. Which of the following is (are) violations of the FINRA Rules of Fair Practice?

I. Churning

II. Selling dividends

III. Performing trades in mutual fund shares

IV. Providing guarantees against losses

A. I and III

B. I and IV

C. III and IV

D. I, II, III, and IV

164. What type of bond is a municipal bond that is quoted at 4.90%?

A. General obligation bond

B. Revenue bond

C. Term bond

D. Serial bond

165. Which of the following statements regarding a municipal broker's broker are correct?

I. The firm may act as agent for other dealers

II. The firm may purchase bonds and place in its inventory

III. The firm may offer bonds to institutional customers

IV. A municipal brokers' broker may be used to protect the anonymity of other dealers

A. I and III

B. I and IV

C. II only

D. I, II, III, and IV

166. Revenues would flow through these accounts in which order under a net revenue pledge?

> I. Reserve maintenance funds
>
> II. Debt service funds
>
> III. Operations and maintenance fund
>
> IV. Surplus fund

A. II, III, I, and IV

B. III, II, I, and IV

C. III, I, II, and IV

D. II, III, IV, and I

167. A trade of 10,000 shares that is announced on the tape after the trade execution on the floor of the exchange is known as what type of trade?

A. Special offer

B. Secondary distribution

C. Specialist's Bid

D. Exchange distribution

168. Which of the following entities issue listed option contracts?

A. The Options Clearing Corporation

B. Broker/dealer firms

C. The writer of the option's contract

D. The exchange where the options are listed

169. A group of investors is interested in the purchase of a new issue municipal bond of Ironwerks city. Where would the investors go to obtain information about the issue?

A. Bond registration statement

B. New issue prospectus

C. Bond official statement

D. Moody's or S&P bond rating service

170. What would happen to municipal bonds that lose their tax-free status?

A. Bond prices would increase

B. Bond yields would increase

C. Bond prices would remain the same

D. Bond yields would decrease

171. XYZ Securities calls ABC Securities for a quote on a bond that ABC Securities offered through an on-line system. XYZ Securities states that the bond is out firm for an hour at 97 to DEF Securities. Which of the following is/are true?

> I. XYZ Securities may purchase the bond immediately at 97
>
> II. If ABC Securities has a ten-minute recall, XYZ Securities may be able to purchase the bond at 95 in ten minutes
>
> III. DEF Securities has an hour to buy the bond at 97 if the option was granted without recall
>
> IV. If DEF Securities decides not to buy the bond, XYZ Securities has first right to buy the bond

A. I and II

B. I, II, and III

C. I, III, and IV

D. II, III, and IV

172. Which of the following bonds would an issuer not be able to issue if an additional bond test exists in the trust indenture?

A. Equivalent lien bonds

B. Junior lien bonds

C. Senior lien bonds

D. The issuer could not issue additional bonds under any circumstances

173. A trade that is a private transaction between the specialist and a public customer is known as what type of trade?

A. Special offer

B. Secondary distribution

C. Specialist's Bid

D. Exchange distribution

174. Which of the following positions is a short straddle?

A. Long call, short put

B. Long call, long put

C. Short call, short put

D. Short call, long put

175. A municipal issuer looking to sell securities through a competitive bid underwriting will publish all of the following EXCEPT:

A. The existence of a good faith deposit

B. The names of the members of the underwriting syndicate

C. Types of bonds (general obligation or revenue bonds)

D. The registration provisions for the bonds

176. Which of the following statements is not true regarding municipal bond quotes?

A. A firm participating in a joint account may imply multiple markets for the security

B. Firms giving quotes to other member firms may not knowingly misrepresent the quote

C. All quotes are assumed to be firm unless otherwise specified

D. Municipal bond quotes may be subject to price change and a prior sale

177. For which of the following would SEC rules on insider trading apply?

A. Company president

B. Investment banker that has access to non-public information

C. A secretary to the company president with access to non-public information

D. All of the above

178. Your customer enters an order for the purchase of XYZ stock at the best available price without specifying the price but expecting execution. What type of order would this be?

A. A market order

B. A limit order

C. A stop order

D. A stop limit order

179. Which of the following is not a purpose of the Securities Act of 1934?

A. Regulate over-the-counter trading

B. Regulation of exchanges

C. Regulation of new security issues

D. Maintenance of a fair and honest marketplace

180. A municipal bond syndicate has $1,000,000 of bonds available for sale to the public. The syndicate manager will fill which of the following orders on the books?

I.	$500,000 member
II.	$500,000 designated
III.	$500,000 group net

A. I and II

B. II and III

C. I and III

D. Proportionate allocation to I, II, and III

181. The purchase of a municipal bond at a premium results in a decrease in the book value of the bond during the period that the bond is held. This process is referred to as:

A. Accretion

B. Accrual

C. Amortization

D. Depreciation

182. Which of the following statements are true in regards to a municipal securities underwriting?

I.	The syndicate manager is the only one with authority to determine the offering's priority
II.	Group orders must disclose the identity of the purchaser from the firm entering the order
III.	The syndicate manager must provide a written statement detailing the syndicate expenses to each of the members of the syndicate

A. I only

B. I and III

C. II and III

D. I, II, and III

183. Investment advisors do not have to register with the SEC when the number of clients they work with is fewer than how many?

    A.   10
    B.   15
    C.   20
    D.   25

184. Trading programs that are commercially available do all of the following EXCEPT:

    A.   Cause investors to act on a nearly simultaneous basis
    B.   Trigger buy and sell signals
    C.   Monitor quotes in real-time
    D.   Create long-term market aberrations

185. Which of the following is not required to be registered in the state before selling securities to its residents?

    A.   A broker-dealer that is resident in the state
    B.   A registered representative that is a resident in the state
    C.   A broker/dealer that is a non-resident of the state
    D.   All of the above must be registered

186. A securities firm is the managing underwriter for an offering of Alameda County bonds. The bonds are to be sold to investors at par. Compensation will flow to members as follows: Syndicate non-member broker-dealers will be able to purchase bonds at $990 and members of the underwriting syndicate may purchase bonds at $984. If syndicate member A purchases 100 bonds and sells them to a non-member, the additional takedown would be:

    A. $6.00
    B. $9.00
    C. $15.00
    D. $24.00

187. Which of the following orders must be approved by a municipal securities principal?

    A.   Solicited orders
    B.   Unsolicited orders
    C.   Discretionary orders
    D.   All of the above

188. Transatlantic Railroad Corp is looking to sell 500,000 shares to the public. 200,000 shares are coming from the company's treasury shares and 300,000 are new shares. This offering would be considered a:

    A.   Initial public offering
    B.   Primary distribution
    C.   Secondary distribution
    D.   Split offering

189. What may a brokerage firm do for a customer who requests that the firm hold fully-paid securities?

    A.   Require that the securities be segregated
    B.   Provide the firm with the request in writing
    C.   Require that the securities be held in a cash account
    D.   Require the customer to provide the firm with stock powers

190. If a corporation declares a dividend for its shareholders of record as of April 12, on what date does the stock begin trading ex-dividend?

    A.   April 9
    B.   April 10
    C.   April 5
    D.   April 12

191. A municipality includes in its Notice of Sale for a new issue of bonds its preference for bidding syndicates to enter their bids based on true-interest-cost. Why would the municipality choose this method?

   A. The IRS prefers the true-interest-cost method

   B. The true-interest-cost is easier to calculate

   C. True-interest-cost is calculated using constant dollars

   D. True-interest-cost is calculated using actual dollar

192. A firm acting as financial advisor for a municipal issuer wishes to participate in a competitive bid underwriting. This may be done provided that:

   I. The firm terminates the advisor relationship with the municipal issuer

   II. The city agrees to the firm's participation in the competitive bid

   III. The financial advisor relationship is disclosed to the customers of the firm

   IV. The firm gives back any compensation received as financial advisor for the municipal issuer

   A. I and III

   B. I, II, and III

   C. II, III, and IV

   D. I, II, III, and IV

193. With what is the term underwriting used in conjunction?

   A. Firms participating in the distribution of a new security issue

   B. Firms participating in the distribution of a secondary issue

   C. Firms acting as a broker in the secondary market

   D. Firms acting as a dealer in the secondary market

194. To which of the following does the FINRA 5% Mark-up Policy apply?

   I. Sales of open-end investment company shares

   II. Sales of common shares through a registered secondary

   III. OTC sales of outstanding nonexempt securities

   A. I only

   B. III only

   C. I and II

   D. I, II, and III

195. What is the maximum time allowed for trade settlement if a bank trust account purchases 100 shares of DEF securities, requiring C.O.D. delivery?

   A. 5 business days

   B. 15 days

   C. 35 days

   D. 60 business days

196. A syndicate member in an undivided account is liable for an unsold balance of new issue municipal securities under what conditions?

   A. Unsold bonds remain in the account

   B. The time limit established for the duration of the account has not yet expired

   C. The member has not sold its pro-rata allotment

   D. All of the above

197. A customer purchases a bond in a state with a restriction on the amount of taxes that can be raised for repayment of the bond. Which of the following would be true of this bond?

   A. The taxation limitation is statutory

   B. The taxation limitation is constitutional

   C. Statutory limitations may be changed by the taxing authority

   D. All of the above

198. A specialist may perform all of the following duties EXCEPT:

A. Act as an underwriter

B. Act as a broker

C. Act as a dealer

D. Handle odd lots

199. If a customer purchases ABC stock in a regular way settlement on Thursday, October 7, what is the settlement date for the transaction?

A. Friday, October 8

B. Monday, October 11

C. Tuesday, October 12

D. Friday, October 15

200. A customer purchases a new issue municipal bond at 96, which matures in 20 years and sells the bond after eight years for 92. What is the gain or loss on the sale?

A. $76 gain

B. $80 gain

C. $40 loss

D. $56 loss

201. Which of the following would be considered an accredited investor?

I.	A banker who received $200,000 in income for the last two years (expects to receive the same this year)
II.	The owner of a business with a net worth in excess of $1,000,000
III.	A lawyer who received $150,000 in income for the last two years and expects to receive this year
IV.	A broker with a net worth of $200,000

A. III and IV

B. II and III

C. I and II

D. I, II, III, and IV

202. Retained earnings represent what on a corporate balance sheet?

A. Shareholder's equity

B. Capital surplus

C. Undistributed net income

D. Working capital

203. A company is being sued for $10 billion. If the company prevails, the stock price will probably increase. If the company is unsuccessful, it may go out of business. The company's stock would be considered:

A. Blue chip

B. Growth

C. Defensive

D. Special situation

204. What is the redemption price of an open-end investment company?

A. NAV + SC

B. NAV

C. POP

D. Determined by the market

205. A customer opens an account with an opening purchase of 300 shares of XYZ @ $60. Subsequently XYZ increases to $64 per share, then decreases to $58 per share. Assuming Regulation T is 50%, the equity and SMA in the account will be which of the following:

A. $8,400 equity; $0 SMA

B. $8,400 equity; $600 SMA

C. $9,000; $0 SMA

D. $10,200 equity; $600 SMA

206. What is the penalty to a customer who withdraws money from an IRA account prior to age 59½ and who is not disabled or suffering from a hardship?

A. 0%

B. 10%

C. 15%

D. 25%

207. Which of the following statements is correct concerning the purchase of open-end investment company shares?

A. The registered representative can receive continuing commissions for selling such shares after the termination of their employment with a FINRA member

B. A Letter of Intent (LOI) for the purchase of shares is valid for a 24-month period after the initial transaction

C. The purchase of open-end investment company shares must be made prior to the payment of a declared dividend

D. Brokers are permitted to arrange for the extension of credit to a customer for the purchase of shares

208. A customer buys a Treasury bond on Tuesday February 23. The payment dates are January 1 and July 1. How many days accrued interest must the customer pay?

A. 54

B. 60

C. 64

D. 70

209. A registered representative of Firm A opens an account for an employee of Firm B. Under FINRA rules:

I. Firm A must send duplicate confirmations and statements to Firm B upon request

II. Firm A must notify Firm B of that the account is being opened for their registered representative

III. The registered representative of Firm B must be informed by Firm A that their employer will be notified of the opening of the account

IV. Firm A must obtain the Firm B's permission for each trade entered in the account

A. IV only

B. I and II

C. I, II, and IV

D. I, II, and III

210. Which of the following bonds would show yield to call on the trade confirmation?

A. 10% nominal yield, 12% yield to maturity

B. 10% nominal yield, 10% yield to maturity

C. 10% nominal yield, 8% yield to maturity

D. 10% nominal yield, 14% yield to maturity

211. The approval of municipal securities advertisement is performed by:

A. MSRB

B. NYSE

C. Principal

D. SEC

212. Which of the following would not be permitted in an ad for variable life insurance?

I. Offered by XYZ Insurance, the recipient of the highest insurance industry ratings

II. You can have quick and easy access to your funds and maintain high rates of return

III. A hypothetical illustration of investment in a variable life insurance policy to investment in term insurance plus a certificate of deposit

IV. Here are the rankings of variable life insurance policies originally published by a national magazine

A. I, II, and III

B. II, III, and IV

C. I, III, and IV

D. I, II, and IV

213. An investor owns 1,000 shares of stock that paid annual dividends of $1.00 per share and 20 corporate bonds that paid nominal interest of 5%. Assuming the investor is in a 25% tax bracket and held the securities all year, how much tax would be due?

A. $300

B. $400

C. $500

D. $1,000

214. A CMO tranche with a stated maturity range and no guarantee of maturity within that range is known as what type of tranche?

    A.   Planned amortization class

    B.   Principal only securities

    C.   Companion class

    D.   Targeted Amortization Class

215. Which of the following is NOT true about self-regulatory organizations (SROs)?

    A.   SROs establish Conduct Rules

    B.   SROs handle trade practice complaints

    C.   SROs file criminal complaints against rule violations

    D.   SROs act as quasi-governmental agencies

216. Which of the following would not be used to support general obligation bonds issued by the state?

    A.   Income taxes

    B.   Gasoline taxes

    C.   DMV licensing fees

    D.   Ad valorem taxes

217. A customer sells 1 ABC July 40 call for $5 per share and buys 1 ABC November 40 call for $8 per share. What is the maximum loss?

    A. $300

    B. $500

    C. $1,300

    D.   Unlimited

218. What is authorized common stock defined as?

    A.   Issued plus treasury stock

    B.   Outstanding plus repurchased stock

    C.   Issued stock minus treasury stock

    D.   The total amount of stock that the corporation can issue according to its charter

219. Which type of government security investment allows an investor to lock in a specific yield without reinvestment risk?

    A.   Treasury bills

    B.   Treasury notes

    C.   Treasury bonds

    D.   Treasury STRIPs

220. Which of the following functions is performed by the custodian of a mutual fund?

    A.   Disbursement of dividend and capital gains distributions

    B.   Safeguard the physical assets of the fund

    C.   Participation in the sales and distribution of fund shares

    D.   Distribution of proxies and periodic reports

221. When evaluating the risk that is involved with investing in a raw land real estate limited partnership, which of the following would not be a consideration?

    A.   Aspects of the program investment that are non-liquid

    B.   Lack of depreciation in the program investment

    C.   The program's economic soundness

    D.   Investment tax credits available to the investment

222. Which of the following are correct regarding variable annuity contracts?

I.	The investor is protected against loss of principal
II.	The annultant receives a monthly or periodic payment that may fluctuate in value
III.	Investment risk is assumed by the issuer of the variable annuity contract
IV.	Control of the variable annuity's principal value is given up by the annultant upon when annultization occurs

    A.   I and II

    B.   I and IV

    C.   II and III

    D.   II and IV

223. A customer is looking to redeem 1,000 shares of mutual fund they purchased. The POP is $15 per share; the SC for the fund is 6%, and the fund has a redemption fee of 1%. What dollar amount will the investor receive upon redemption?

   A. $13,959

   B. $14,100

   C. $14,241

   D. $14,650

224. A company is calling its bonds at 105, which are convertible at $25 per share. The company's common stock is trading at $28 per share. Which of the following statements is correct?

I.	The common stock's parity price is $25
II.	This would create a forced conversion
III.	The bondholders should convert their bonds
IV.	The bondholders should allow the bonds to be called

   A. I and IV

   B. II and III

   C. IV only

   D. I, II, and IV

225. Which of the following statements is (are) true according to the FINRA Code of Arbitration?

I.	A dispute between two firms must be decided through arbitration
II.	A dispute between a registered representative and a broker/dealer must go through arbitration
III.	The decision of an arbitrator is not subject to appeal
IV.	A customer may force a broker/dealer into arbitration

   A. I and II

   B. II, III, and IV

   C. I and IV

   D. I, II, III, and IV

226. Which of the following statements is incorrect regarding seller's option settlement?

   A. They may not be settled prior to the sixth business day after trade date (T+6)

   B. They must be settled by the 60th day after trade date (T+60)

   C. The seller may choose to settle before the specified date with a written notice of at least two days to the buyer

   D. The seller may not settle the trade prior to the specified date

227. Which of the following functions will a SIPC trustee perform in sequence?

I.	Distribute identifiable customer property
II.	Handle all SIPC claims
III.	Verify the records of brokerage firm
IV.	Make notification to customers

   A. IV, I, III, and II

   B. III, IV, I, and II

   C. IV, III, II, and I

   D. IV, III, I, and II

228. An investor who bought 100 shares of stock in January @ $20 a share and sold the stock in August for $30 a share would owe how much in taxes (assuming the investor is in a 25% tax bracket)?

   A. $100

   B. $150

   C. $200

   D. $250

229. MSRB rules limit gifts to no more than:

   A. $200

   B. $100

   C. $50

   D. Gifts are not permitted under MSRB rules

230. A registered representative of Firm XYZ sells a hot issue to a registered representative of Firm ABC. Which person is liable for violating the free-riding and withholding rules?

I.	Firm ABC
II.	Firm XYZ
III.	The registered representative of Firm XYZ
IV.	The registered representative of Firm ABC

A. I and III

B. I and II

C. III and IV

D. I, II, III, and IV

231. CMOs that have been issued with several tranches, varying maturities, and that retire sequentially, are often described as:

A. Vanilla CMOs

B. Serial CMOs

C. Series CMOs

D. Sequential CMOs

232. A customer sells 1 ABC July 40 call for $5 per share and buys 1 ABC November 40 call for $8 per share. What is this type of option strategy called?

A. Straddle

B. Spread

C. Combination

D. Exercise

233. A stock certificate held in street name has what name on the certificate?

A. The broker/dealer's name

B. The shareholder's name

C. The name of the registrar's

D. The transfer agent's name

234. A customer buys an American Aviation Corp 10% bond at 105 that matures in ten years. What is the current yield?

A. 9.27%

B. 9.52%

C. 9.76%

D. 11.22%

235. What is the sales load for an open-end investment company that has a bid price of $14.35 and an offering price of $15.50?

A. 7.00%

B. 7.42%

C. 8.22%

D. 8.50%

236. Which of the following is not considered to be a conflict of interest with respect to a limited partnership?

A. The general partner accepts $50,000 to not compete with the limited partnership

B. The general partner selling an existing office building owned by the general partner to the limited partnership

C. The general partner acting as agent for the partnership and managing partnership assets

D. The general partner accepting a loan directly from the limited partnership

237. Which type of account is used in connection with a variable annuity?

A. Special

B. Margin

C. Separate

D. General

238. A customer wants to invest $60,000 in three income funds with different investment management firms. Which of the following should the customer understand about the investment?

- A. That withdrawal programs are available
- B. Dividends and distributions will be automatically reinvestment
- C. The fund has exchange privileges
- D. There will be sales charge breakpoints available

239. The preferred stock of a company is trading at 102, convertible into common stock at $50 per share. What is the parity price of the common stock?

- A. $2.04
- B. $50.00
- C. $51.00
- D. $0.19

240. Credit on a new issue may not be extended by a broker/dealer participating in the distribution of the issue for how long?

- A. Within 30 days prior to transaction
- B. Within 60 days prior to transaction
- C. Within 90 days prior to transaction
- D. Within 120 days before or after transaction

241. All of the following statements regarding SIPC are true, EXCEPT:

- A. SIPC protects consumers in the event of a broker/dealer's insolvency
- B. SIPC's funding comes from assessments on member firms
- C. SIPC is a non-profit corporation
- D. SIPC is a U.S. government agency

242. What is meant when a technical analyst states that the market is "consolidating"?

- A. Moving downward
- B. Moving upward
- C. Moving sideways
- D. Reversing an upward trend

243. A convertible bond has a conversion ratio of 20. The bond is selling in the market for $800. What is the parity price of the stock?

- A. $20
- B. $40
- C. $50
- D. $80

244. A customer enters an order to buy 1,000 XYZ at 38 or 42 Stop. He receives a report that he bought 700 shares at $38 per share. What order remains on the book?

- A. Buy 300 at 38 or buy 1,000 at 42 Stop
- B. Buy 300 at 38 or buy 300 at 42 Stop
- C. Buy 1,000 at 38 or 300 at 42 Stop
- D. The balance is canceled; no order remains

245. Which of the following is considered the firm quote?

- A. Bid 14 Asked 14.50
- B. Bid 14 Asked 14.50 Subject
- C. Bid 14 Asked 14.50 Workout
- D. All of the above

246. If the bond counsel issues a statement that there is no question regarding the terms of a municipality's bond offering or the issuer's authority to borrow funds, the statement is considered to be:

- A. A qualified opinion
- B. An opinion issued by a qualified attorney
- C. An opinion that states that the issuer has clear title to the financed facility
- D. An unqualified opinion

247. If you wanted to know the dollar amount of a new bond issue coming out in 20 days from the City of Chicago, you would find this information in the:

- A. Bond Buyer's 20 Bond Index
- B. Bond Buyer's 30 Bond Index
- C. Revenue Bond Index
- D. Visible Supply

248. A customer (with no securities positions) sells 1 ABC September 30 put for a premium of $3, when the price of ABC stock is $30 per share. What is the customer's maximum loss?

A. $300

B. $2,700

C. $3,000

D. Unlimited

249. ACME Electronics has a 7% cumulative preferred stock outstanding. Four years ago, the company paid a dividend of $5 per share. Three years ago, the company paid a dividend of $6 per share. Two years ago, the company paid a dividend of $7 per share. How much in dividends did the company pay preferred stockholders before it paid a dividend to the common stockholders last year?

A. $0 per share

B. $7 per share

C. $10 per share

D. $14 per share

250. Bonds of the Federal Farm Credit Consolidated System-wide are:

I.	Taxable on the federal return
II.	Taxable on state and local returns
III.	Secured by farm mortgage pools
IV.	Backed and guaranteed by the U.S. Government

A. I only

B. II and III

C. I and IV

D. I, II, and III

1. B.

A put is out-of-the-money when the market price is higher than the strike price; a call goes out-of-the-money when the market price is below the strike price.

2. C.

Accrued interest is calculated beginning from the last payment date up to but not including the date of settlement, which is three business days after the trade date (T+3). For corporate bonds, months are assumed to have 30 days. There will be thirty days each for the months of January and February. The settlement date of the trade will be March 23, barring weekends or holidays. There will be 22 days of accrued interest for the month of March, for a total of 82 days (30 + 30 + 22). The accrued interest will be $18.22, as follows: $1,000 \times 8\% \times 82 / 360$.

3. C.

Cumulative voting allows the customer to direct votes and influence the office of his choice. The total number of votes available would be 1,200 (600 shares × 2 offices).

4. A.

The call is in-the-money (+11) so it would be exercised (the put would expire worthless) resulting in a gain of $1,100 for exercising the call and a loss of $600 in total premiums paid for a net profit of $500.

5. D.

Warrants carry a longer term than rights with a subscription price that is above the market price.

6. C.

The break even is the strike price of the long call ($40) plus the debit ($3) or $40 + $3 = $43.

7. D.

Because the municipal bonds are purchased in the secondary market at a discount to par, there is no adjustment (accretion) for the purchaser's cost. The gain on sale would be the difference between the sale price ($1,030) less the original cost ($970), or $60.

8. D.

The combined premiums received as a credit represents the maximum gain.

9. A.

A purchase of Treasury bills has a minimum purchase amount of $10,000 and is issued at a discount to par. T-bill maturities are three, six, or nine months.

10. C.

Income stocks tend to come from mature companies in stable industries.

11. A.

The maximum potential loss for a put writer is the strike price less the premium received.

12. D.

Jointly registered certificates must be signed by both parties the way they appear on the certificate.

13. D.

The MSRB (Municipal Securities Rulemaking Board) is responsible for self-regulation, rule-making, and education among its principal duties in the municipal securities market. Enforcement powers are delegated to the U.S. Securities and Exchange Commission (SEC), Financial Industry Regulatory Authority (FINRA), Office of the Comptroller of Currency (OCC), Federal Deposit Insurance Corporation (FDIC), and Federal Reserve System (FRS).

14. A.

Common stock allows the shareholder to receive a pro rata share of dividends issued and vote for members of the board of directors.

15. C.

Debentures are backed by the full faith and credit of the issuer.

16. C.

$6.03 (offering price) × 300 shares = $1,809 which includes the sales charge or commission.

17. D.

A U.S. Government guarantee for GNMA securities ensures the timely payment of both principal and interest.

18. B.

Inactive accounts receive statements on a quarterly basis, unless there are options trades, in which statements are sent monthly.

19. C.

Under Regulation T, the margin requirement is 50%.

20. A.

The difference between the ASK and the BID for an OTC market maker is a price spread. As an issue becomes more active (heavily traded), the spread between ASK-BID narrows.

21. D.

The bond's denomination has no benefit on portfolio diversification.

22. B.

To determine the parity price of the stock, take the par value of the bond and divide by price per share ($1,000 ÷ $50 = 20). Upon conversion, the customer will receive 20 shares of common stock. Take the market price of the convertible bond ($975) and divide by the number of shares into which the bond can be converted (20). The parity price equals $48.75.

23. C.

Bondholders do not receive dividends. A sinking fund may be used to redeem bonds, repurchase bonds in the open market or exercise a partial call.

24. B.

"3s" indicates a trade for 300 shares.

25. B.

Mortgage loans to farmers are made by the Federal Land Bank Associations.

26. B.

The Trust Indenture Act of 1939 deals with the offer of corporate bonds in more than one state or on an interstate basis.

27. C.

Capitalization is the chief difference between open-end and closed-end investment companies. Open-end funds (referred to as mutual funds) continuously issue new shares for investors; closed-end funds (referred to as publicly traded funds) trade in the secondary market similar to corporate stocks.

28. D.

Income from a variable annuity will vary and is not fixed (as in with a fixed annuity); this may be of concern for an individual who is dependent upon a certain level of monthly income in retirement.

29. B.

Market risk (also known as systematic risk) is the risk that a security may lose value due to a decline in the market.

30. D.

The transaction requires a transfer agent and the registrar to receipt and transfer ownership of the shares between the old and new owner.

31. B.

Keogh plans are tax-qualified retirement plans that provide for the deferral of taxes on the inside accumulation of value until retirement.

32. D.

The investment objectives of a mutual fund can take place with the approval of more than 50% of the fund's shareholders.

33. B.

Preferred stock does not provide a guaranteed dividend; when dividends are issued and paid, they are based on a fixed (stated) rate.

34. C.

Funds that carry a load (sales charge) and no-load funds are permitted to charge 12b-1 distribution fees, provided for no-load funds, the distribution fee does not exceed ¼ of 1% of net assets. The distribution fee is an annual expense charged to shareholders.

35. B.

The maximum penalty under the Summary Complaint Procedure for FINRA is a censure and a fine of up to $2,500.

36. A.

The Bond Buyer's 11 Bond Index, which consists of 11 of the 20 highest rated general obligation municipal bonds found in the 20 Bond Index, would have a lower yield.

37. C.

The price per share that an investor receives upon redemption is NAV less sales charge for the sales redemption price.

38. D.

All of the options listed are potential disadvantages of investing in an equipment-leasing program.

39. D.

The customer must pay the execution price for the trade.

40. C.

The pink sheets provide a list of stock prices held by market makers that are not listed on the NASDAQ.

41. C.

Because there is an anti-dilution clause in the trust indenture, the conversion price of the stock would be reduced proportionately. The 10% stock dividend would be incorporated into the share price by increasing the conversion factor to 1.1 and dividing the conversion price of $25 for a new conversion price of $22.72.

42. D.

The writer received $300 in premiums from the sale of the naked put (maximum gain), but lost $500 when ABC fell to $25 per share. $500 – $300 = $200 loss.

43. C.

LMV ($5,000) minus DB ($2,500) = EQ ($2,500).

44. B.

The credit received is the maximum gain.

45. C.

The Uniform Gifts to Minors Act is commonly known as UGMA.

46. A.

All or none (AON) is a type of underwriting or an order qualifier on certain types of securities orders. Bond anticipation notes (BANs), project notes (PNs), and revenue anticipation notes (RANs) are all short-term municipal notes.

47. B.

Qualified private activity bonds are taxable under the alternative minimum tax.

48. D.

The result of the opening transactions are $800 debit – $500 credit = $300 debit. The result of the closing transactions are $800 debit – $500 credit = $300 debit.

49. D.

Any mail of a customer may not be sent to the home of a registered representative.

50. C.

A person that is not registered is not permitted to give advice regarding municipal securities.

51. D.

The statements made in Choice A, B, and C would be improper and would not be approved by a branch office manager or principal of the firm.

52. A.

The tangible net asset value of a stock is the same as its book value.

53. B.

Variable annuities, unlike fixed annuities, are not guaranteed as to capital loss due to a decrease in the market value of the underlying investments held in the separate account.

54. D.

An individual who is self-employed, participating in an employer-sponsored plan not covered by a second employer, and an individual not covered by their corporate sponsored plan may establish an IRA.

55. D.

More predictable and steadier cash flow is an advantage that CMOs have to GNMAs.

56. B.

($8.50 (A) - $7.80 (B)) ÷ $8.50 (A) = 8.20% sales load (SC).

57. C.

Customer securities at the time of a SIPC liquidation are based on the prevailing market value at that time.

58. B.

Accrued interest on a bond sold by Investor B to Investor A is paid by the seller, Investor B.

59. A.

If the price of the stock went up, the purchaser would not exercise the option and would only lose the $500 premium.

60. A.

I and III are information that are required in a ranking ad.

61. D.

Options are available on all of these types of securities.

62. D.

The bond counsel will perform a review of each of the choices when rendering an opinion on the legality of the bond issue.

63. B.

Long straddles are positions when a put and call on the same underlying security are purchased with the same expiration and same strike price.

64. B.

The XZY trade was a round lot (100 shares) at $8.25 per share.

65. C.

Rule 505 offerings may raise up to $5,000,000.

66. A.

Under the Investment Advisers Act of 1940, an investment adviser is compensated by way of fees, typically a percentage of a client's assets under management. Commissions are paid to brokers who are registered with a broker/dealer pursuant to the Securities Exchange Act of 1934.

67. A.

The life annuity payment option represents the largest potential payout to the holder of a variable annuity contract.

68. C.

A specialist is responsible for maintaining a fair and orderly market in specified stocks on the floor of the exchange.

69. C.

Since investment grade bonds are relatively safe from default (due to high credit ratings), the chief risk is the impact of inflation on the buying power of the bond's proceeds.

70. B.

An analysis of the cash flow will provide information concerning the revenues and expenses of the limited partnership.

71. C.

A long margin account can become restricted if it falls below the initial Regulation T requirement of 50% but remains above the NYSE minimum maintenance requirement of 25%.

72. C.

Choices A, B, and D are fixed value investments that are susceptible to inflation risk, while variable annuity accumulation units fall and rise based on the performance of the securities held in the separate account, providing a better potential hedge against inflation.

73. B.

A firm may institute a policy for the maintenance of broker errors; however there it is no regulatory requirement for the maintenance of such records.

74. C.

A transaction in foreign securities is accomplished through the purchase of ADRs, which are foreign company shares held on deposit in the U.S. If an investor purchases an unregistered ADR, resale may be difficult.

75. B.

A person whose duties are solely clerical in nature would not be required to register as a representative.

76. A.

Agency debt securities typically have higher yields than other securities of the U.S. Government and are not direct obligations of the federal government. FNMA, not GNMA, is a publicly traded corporation listed on the NYSE.

77. B.

Options, stock purchases, and the purchase of mutual fund shares may all be performed in a cash account. Because the short sale of a stock requires the hypothecation of securities on loan from the broker/dealer (or another account), this transaction may only be accomplished in a margin account.

78. D.

The purchase of an instructed number of shares by the registered representative does not require written discretionary authorization.

79. B.

A seller of a put is obligated to purchase the underlying stock at the prevailing market price. This has the potential for an unlimited loss for the put writer as the market price can grow infinitely (theoretically).

80. D.

A firm participating in an underwriting for an issuer must disclose this information on all confirmations and research reports for a period of two years.

81. A.

The parity price of the common stock can be determined by dividing the call price ($102) by the number of shares of common stock into which the preferred stock is convertible (4 shares), equaling $25.50. Since the common stock is trading at $20 per share, you would advise the shareholder to allow the preferred stock to be called, resulting in 4 shares valued higher than the prevailing market value.

82. B.

The break even for a short put is the strike price ($30) – the premium received ($3), which equals $27.

83. B.

Municipal bonds settle in three days (T+3).

84. B.

The offer price or Ask is higher than the net asset value or bid price. To determine the amount, take the NAV and divide it by 100% minus the sales load percentage. For this example, $16.50 ÷ (100% - 8% or 92%) = $17.93.

85. D.

The maximum loss is the combined premiums paid ($400/call + $200/put = $600).

86. D.

The order or preference for corporate securities, in the case of a liquidation, include secured debt (mortgage bonds), unsecured debt (debentures), preferred stock, and common stock.

87. C.

The position is a short straddle. The price of ABC fell to $19 causing the put holder to issue an exercise notice. The writer will purchase the stock at $30 per share ($3,000) and only be able to get $19 ($1,900) resulting in a loss of $1,100. Premiums of $8 ($800) were received for a net loss of $300.

88. C.

If the price of the stock goes to $43 (just prior to or after the expiration of the ABC July 40 call), the holder may exercise the ABC November 40 call resulting in no gain.

89. C.

In order to get the best price execution for a stock that is not listed on NASDAQ, a firm must contact at least three of the market makers listed in the NASDAQ Pink Sheets to obtain quotes.

90. D.

The names of the syndicate members will not appear on the Notice of Sale because the syndicate has not yet been formed when this is first published. The Notice of Sale is used to solicit bids from firms who will form a syndicate.

91. B.

The registered representative has engaged in the sale of a security without the permission of the broker/dealer, which is known as "selling away" and violates FINRA rules.

92. C.

Unless otherwise specified, trades settle based on a regular-way settlement, which is three business days after trade date.

93. D.

The sale of a hot issue to the spouse of a registered representative may take place, provided such purchase is for an insubstantial amount of shares and such purchase is in line with their normal investment practice. Such a purchase (since a hot issue only becomes hot after the initial offering when trading takes place in the secondary market) must be held for investment purposes and not sold for profit taking, which would then constitute a violation of the free-riding and withholding rules.

94. C.

Open-end mutual fund shares are purchased for the ASK price, which was $15. Redemption of the shares takes place at the NAV ($19). This resulted in a per share capital gain of $4 per share that took place within the year, resulting in a short term capital gains taxation at the investor's ordinary income tax rate.

95. C.

Securities issued by the Federal Home Loan Bank are not backed by mortgage pools.

96. B.

The bond interest payments are based on par value, which is $1,000. Since interest payments for corporate bonds are made on a semi-annual basis, the payment will be $50 (10% of $1,000).

97. C.

Financial statements must be issued no less than semi-annually.

98. C.

This strategy is known as "straddling the market" which is a neutral position that allows the investor to gain through the receipt of the call and put premiums.

99. B.

A put gives the purchaser the right to sell a stock at the exercise price. If the stock goes to 0, the purchaser will buy the stock at 0, sell it at 40, and receive $4,000 minus the $5 premium equals $3,500.

100. A.

Limited partners of a limited partnership have the right to inspect the books and records of the partnership and seek legal redress against the general partner for improperly handling proceeds associated with the limited partnership.

101. D.

Prior preferred stock is given priority for dividends and in liquidation order over common and preferred stock.

102. D.

A bond counsel will render an opinion on the tax status of the bonds, the bond issue's validity, and treasury arbitrage regulations. Reoffering yields would not be a consideration in rendering the opinion of the bond counsel.

103. C.

This strategy is a bullish put spread, creating a credit when the long put is purchased for $4 and the short put is sold for $8 ($8 − $4 = $4). The difference between the strike prices ($85 − $75 = $10) less the credit equals the maximum loss, which is $10 − $4 = $600.

104. B.

The symbol "ss" shows that the stock traded in a round lot of 10 shares each so 3 × 10 shares = 30 shares.

105. B.

Initial margin requirements for Reg. T is 50% and the minimum maintenance under NYSE rules is 25%.

106. C.

UITs are unmanaged trusts that invest in fixed income securities such as federal government and/or municipal debt.

107. D.

The management and advisory fees for a money market fund are the largest operating expense.

108. C.

The purpose of illustrated rates of returns in sales literature for variable life insurance is to provide customers with a sense of how their death benefit and cash value may be affected.

109. B.

Regulation T deals with the extension of credit between brokers/dealers and their customers.

110. B.

Whenever an investor buys a municipal bond at a premium, the premium must always be amortized.

111. C.

When interest rates change, it will affect the price of long-term bonds more than short-term bonds. The bonds maturing in ten years will have the greatest price change, as they have the longest-term maturity.

112. A.

The break even for a call is the strike price plus the premium paid ($25 + $3 = $28).

113. B.

An individual participating in an employer-sponsored qualified retirement plan may also contribute to an individual retirement account under the provisions of the Tax Reform Act of 1986. The individual would not be able to deduct contributions from his gross income.

114. C.

GNMAs have the backing of the full faith and credit of the U.S. Government, and there is virtually no default risk.

115. B.

NASDAQ Level I shows the inside market for a stock that consists of the highest bid and the lowest asked price.

116. C.

Choices A, B, and D would likely be financed with revenue bonds and be paid for by user fees; a school construction project would be financed with a general obligation bonds funded with ad valorem taxes.

117. B.

A research report prepared by a registered representative for distribution to customers must be submitted to and approved by a principal of the firm as well as a supervisory analyst prior to its distribution.

118. A.

A commission or mark-up may not be based on the business expenses of the firm but the other factors may be considered.

119. B.

Common and preferred stock has no fixed maturity date.

120. B.

If the customer has the ability to purchase rights the stock is trading ex rights as the market price is adjusted for the value of the rights. One right in this offering is $0.67 (subscription price $45 minus market price $43 / $3 = $0.67). Since the rights are trading for more than this value, the market price of the stock must go to $46 or higher.

121. D.

This situation describes a discretionary transaction, which requires written authorization from the customer prior to the execution of their verbal instruction.

122. C.

When the customer purchased the bond, the yield to maturity was greater than the coupon rate meaning that bond was purchased at a discount to par. When the customer sold the bond, the yield to maturity was less than the nominal yield, meaning that the bond is trading above par or at a premium. Because the customer purchased the bond at a discount and sold it at a premium, there would be a gain on the transaction.

123. A.

A put short spread is bullish on the market and creates a credit between the sale and purchase of the puts.

124. D.

This strategy is a bullish and creates a debit ($6 paid – $3 received = $3 debit).

125. A.

A municipal bond purchased at a premium would result in the cost of the premium being amortized (spread out) over the life of the bond. If held to maturity, there would be no gain or loss at maturity.

126. A.

As the price of ABC rose to $45, the call holder (who is 15 points in-the-money) will issue an exercise notice. The writer will purchase the stock at $45 per share ($4,500) and sell ABC stock for $30 per share ($3,000) resulting in a loss of $1,500. Premiums of $8 ($800) were received as a credit for net loss of $700 (the put would expire worthless).

127. D.

The customer looking for an investment in tax-free municipal bonds may invest in all of the choices.

128. D.

One mill is the equivalent of 0.001; $1,000,000 × 0.005 = $5,000.

129. C.

The maximum profit for the holder of a put is the strike price less the premium paid.

130. D.

The firm holding XYZ stock has backed away from the firm quote of $15 for the stock.

131. C.

All of the choices listed must be disclosed by broker/dealers, except for interest rates on margin debit balance.

132. C.

An increase in the share price of an investment is referred to as a price appreciation.

133. C.

Treasury bonds have a maturity that is more than ten years.

134. B.

The FINRA cannot impose criminal penalties on a member or its representatives.

135. B.

The $6 is the stated dividend (yield), which means this is a non-par preferred stock.

136. C.

A registered representative may be permitted to open a joint account with a public customer and share in the profits with the permission of the firm and only to the extent of their interest in the account.

137. C.

In a long margin account, where the purchase is made, the long market value (LMV) is $10,000; a debit (DB) of 50% or $5,000, which is the Reg. T requirement, is created. Subtracting DB from LMV yields equity of $5,000. When the market value of the convertible bonds increases to 110, the LMV rises to $11,000. Since it only takes $5,500 to meet Reg. T requirements, an excess equity of $500 is created and credited to the Special Memorandum Account (SMA).

138. B.

A state requires that a certificate of limited partnership be filed to establish a limited partnership.

139. C.

Geographical diversification is a strategy that may protect an investor from the effects of Choices A, B, and D. Interest rate risk effects all bonds, regardless of their geographic location.

140. D.

Each of the statements regarding recommendations made by FINRA members is correct.

141. B.

Fees to a firm's customers must be fair and reasonable and not unfairly discriminatory between its customers.

142. A.

The maximum gain to the call writer is the premium; the maximum loss is unlimited.

143. A.

For trades that are 10,000 shares or more the zeros are shown on the tape using a decimal instead of a comma as a separator. "SLD" indicates that the trade was reported out of sequence.

144. D.

Instinet is an agency only broker trading system for institutional investors that execute trades without the services of a broker/dealer. These trades occur in the fourth market.

145. C.

Municipal bond interest is exempt from federal income; if the purchaser lives in the locality where the bonds are issued, the bonds are also exempt from local taxes (double-tax exempt).

146. D.

Because the customer bought and sold the securities the same day for the same amount, there is no net amount subject to margin requirements when calculated at the end of the day.

147. C.

CMOs with three tranches will retire the shortest maturity first by paying interest and principal until it is retired.

148. D.

The joint life annuity payment option ensures that payments will continue to the survivor upon the death of the first tenant (typically a spouse).

149. C.

Firms are permitted to sell hot issues of their securities to their employees.

150. D.

The broker/dealer is the only entity listed that cannot authenticate a security that has been mutilated.

151. B.

Because high yield bonds have a high potential for default, they would not be purchased by a fiduciary under the Prudent Man Rule.

152. C.

Bonds that are deemed investment grade have ratings that are AAA, AA, A, or BBB. Bonds that are rated C or lower would be considered speculative grade.

153. B.

A fixed number of annuity units will be received by the annuitant based on the value of the accumulation units upon annuitization.

154. B.

Official statements are provided to ensure that disclosure requirements for retail customers are met.

155. A.

An officer of the issuer may NOT in any way act as purchaser's representative in the transaction.

156. A.

Annuities, which are issued by insurance companies, involve the inside accumulation of assets over time that is tax deferred. All other examples generate taxable income, unless held in a tax-qualified plan.

157. D.

Face amount certificates, unit investment trusts, and publicly-traded funds (also referred to as close-end investment companies) are all referred in the Investment Company Act of 1940 as investment companies. A holding company is a form of corporate ownership.

158. D.

Warrants represent a future intent to purchase new issue shares of the underlying stock. Until exercised, there is no stock to issue dividends.

159. C.

Third market trades must be reported within 90 seconds in accordance with FINRA rules.

160. A.

Regardless of the firm's allotted share of the underwriting or whether the firm sold its allotment, each member would be responsible for their pro-rata share of the unsold bonds. In this example, the firm is responsible for 20% of the unsold bonds or $60,000 (this is known as an Eastern Account or undivided account underwriting).

161. D.

Coterminous entities share the same taxing boundaries. Since such entities rely on the same revenue sources (i.e. taxpayers) to service their respective debts, this would be overlapping debt.

162. B.

A floor broker performs order executions for member firms.

163. D.

Each of the choices listed are considered violations of FINRA's Rules of Fair Practice.

164. D.

Bonds that are quotes as 1/10th of a percent are characteristic of serial bonds, which are quoted on a yield to maturity basis.

165. B.

Municipal broker's brokers work on the behalf of other dealers, not public customers or institutions and are often used to protect the anonymity of these dealers.

166. B.

With a net revenue pledge, the money would go first to the Operation and Maintenance Fund, followed by the Debt Service, Reserve Maintenance Fund, and finally to the Surplus Fund.

167. D.

A large block trade of 10,000 shares or more would be reported on the tape after trade completion would be an exchange distribution.

168. A.

Listed options contracts are standardized and issued by the Options Clearing Corporation.

169. C.

The bond's official statement would provide investors with information about a new issue municipal bond, in a similar way a prospectus provides information about a new issue corporate security. Remember, municipal bonds are exempt from the registration requirements pursuant to the Securities Act of 1933.

170. A.

Municipal bonds that lose their tax free status would cause those bonds to be less valuable then municipal bonds that have tax-free status. A drop in bond prices would result in an increase in bonds yields.

171. D.

DEF Securities has the first right to purchase the bond unless ABC Securities has a ten-minute recall provision in which case ABC Securities may recall the bond giving DEF Securities ten minutes to enter the buy order; if there is no ten-minute recall, DEF Securities has one hour to enter the order. If DEF Securities decides not to purchase the bond, XYZ Securities obtains first right to buy it.

172. A.

If an additional bond test exists in the trust indenture, the issuer may be able to sell both junior and equivalent lien bonds. It would not have the ability to issue senior lien bonds under any circumstances.

173. C.

A trade that is a private transaction between a specialist and public customer is known as a specialist's bid.

174. C.

The sale of a call and put on the same security with the same strike price and expiration date is called a short straddle. It is a neutral position for a market that is moving sideways where the customer is looking to profit from the premiums received.

175. B.

When the Notice of Sale is published, it will not have yet formed the underwriting syndicate therefore such information will not be included.

176. A.

A municipal securities firm participating in a joint account may not imply multiple markets for the municipal security.

177. D.

Any individual with access to non-public information would be subject to the provisions of the Insider Trading and Securities Fraud Enforcement Act of 1988.

178. A.

Market orders are the only type of order that guarantees immediate execution at the next available price in the market.

179. C.

New issues are regulated through the Securities Act of 1933 (also known as the New Issues or Prospectus Act). The Securities Exchange Act of 1934 regulates the trading of securities in the secondary markets, including exchanges and over-the-counter, as well as broker, dealers and registered representatives (also referred to as the Secondary Trading Act).

180. B.

The order sequence for a municipal bond offering through a syndicate is pre-sale, group net, designated, and member. The group net order would be filled first followed by the designated order for $500,000 each. There would be no bonds remaining for the member order of $500,000.

181. C.

The cost of the bond's premium is being amortized over the holding period.

182. C.

Statements II and III are correct. Statement I would not be correct because the priority order of sales is set by the syndicate, not the syndicate manager solely.

183. B.

Under the provisions of the Investment Advisers Act of 1940, a person who gives investment advice for a fee to more than 15 persons is required to register with the SEC as an investment advisors (keep in mind that some states may have a lower de minimus standard for number of clients).

184. D.

Commercially available trading programs may create short-term, but not long-term, aberrations in trading patterns.

185. D.

Regardless of domicile all broker/dealers and registered representatives doing business in the state must be registered.

186. A.

The syndicate member would receive $15 for their purchase ($1000 - $985 = $15) and give back the difference between the selling and the concession received ($1000 - $991 = $9; $15 - $9 = $6).

187. D.

All municipal securities orders must be approved by a municipal securities principal.

188. D.

The offering described in the question is a split offering since it includes a primary distribution of new shares and a secondary distribution of previously issued treasury shares.

189. B.

A request by a customer for a brokerage firm to hold the customer's fully paid securities must be done in writing.

190. B.

The ex-dividend date is two business days prior to the record date.

191. C.

True-interest-cost is calculated using constant dollars, which accounts for the net present value of interest payments made to investors.

192. B.

All of the choices are correct except for choice IV. There is no requirement for the firm to give back any compensation that it has already earned in its prior advisory relationship with the municipal issuer.

193. A.

An underwriting is the distribution of a new issue of securities.

194. B.

FINRA 5% Mark-up Policy deals with the sale of nonexempt OTC securities that are outstanding.

195. C.

C.O.D. (DVP or delivery versus payment) must be settled within 35 calendar days.

196. A.

For members in an undivided account (also known as an Eastern Account), liability remains as long as unsold bonds remain in the account.

197. D.

All of these statements are true regarding bonds that are known as limited tax rate bonds.

198. A.

A specialist performs all of the listed duties except participate in underwritings.

199. C.

Because the common stock is settling in a regular-way, the settlement is T+3 (trade date plus 3 business days).

200. D.

The bond, which is an original issue discount (OID) bond, must be accreted (interest earned would be the difference between par - $1,000 - and the OID, which was $960). Holding the bond to maturity would result in $40 earned over the 20 year period ($2 per year). The bond was held for eight years, for a total accretion of $16, which is added to the original cost. The difference between the sale price ($920) and cost as adjusted ($976) would be a $56 loss to the seller.

201. C.

An accredited investor is a person with net income of $200,000 or more for the last two years, who expects that much this year, or a net worth of $1,000,000 or more.

202. C.

On the balance sheet retained earnings are a component of shareholder's equity or net worth (Total Equity minus Total Liabilities equals Shareholder's Equity), which is the undistributed portion of net income retained by the company. Other components of equity include par value of preferred stock, par value of common stock and paid-in capital additions.

203. D.

The uncertainty of the company's fate due to the lawsuit makes the stock highly speculative and subject to a special situation that will influence its future price.

204. B.

The net asset value (Bid) is the price received when redeeming shares of an open-end investment company.

205. B.

In a long margin account, where the purchase is made, the long market value (LMV) is $18,000; a debit (DB) of 50% or $9,000, which is the Reg. T requirement, is created. Subtracting DB from LMV yields equity of $9,000. When the market value increases to $64 per share, the LMV rises to $19,200. Since it only takes $9,600 to meet Reg. T requirements, the excess $600 in equity created is credited to the Special Memorandum Account (SMA). Once SMA credited, it does not diminish unless the customer uses the balance. When the LMV of XYZ drops to $58 per share, the account value falls to $17,400. DB remains unchanged and the equity falls by $1,800 to $8,400. SMA is unaffected at $600.

206. A.

An individual who makes a withdrawal from an IRA account prior to age 59½ will be subject to a penalty of 10%, with the distribution treated as ordinary income for tax purposes.

207. A.

Under a written agreement with the FINRA member, a registered representative can receive continuing commissions for selling mutual fund shares even after they cease employment with the member. Selling dividends is an unfair trade practice and mutual funds are not eligible as marginable securities. An investor's intent to purchase additional shares of a fund in order to qualify for a quantity discount (breakpoint) must take place within 13 months after the initial purchase under a Letter of Intent.

208. A.

Accrued interest on U.S. Government securities goes from the last payment date up to, but not including settlement date, based on actual calendar days with a T+1 settlement (trade date plus one). There will be 31 days accrued interest for the month of January. The settlement date will be Wednesday, February 24, so there will be 23 days of accrued interest for February, for a total of 54 days.

209. D.

Under FINRA rules, a registered representative must obtain permission to open an account away from their firm. Duplicate trade confirmations and statements must be provided to the registered representative's broker/dealer upon request and the registered representative must be informed that their broker/dealer will be notified regarding the opening of the account.

210. C.

The yield to call would be the lowest for a bond that is trading at a premium. A bond with a nominal yield of 10% and 8% yield to maturity would be trading at a premium, because the yield is less than the stated or coupon rate. Choice A is trading at a discount, because the yield is greater than the coupon rate.

211. C.

Municipal securities advertisement, in accordance with MSRB Rule G-21(f), is approved by the firm's securities principal (municipal or general) and maintained by the firm. Neither the NYSE, the SEC, nor MSRB approve municipal securities advertisement.

212. A.

Choices I, II, and III would not be permitted in a variable life insurance ad. Choice IV may be permitted provided that the ranking information is presented in a proper form.

213. B.

The tax due on the dividends paid would be 15% of $1,000 ($150). Bond interest would be taxed as ordinary income, which is calculated at $20,000 × 5% = $1,000 × 25% = $250. $150 + $250 = $400.

214. D.

The maturity time for TACs may go beyond the CMOs estimated range.

215. C.

Self-regulatory organizations have no criminal prosecutorial powers.

216. D.

Ad valorem taxes are typically taxes that counties and cities levy on property, which is not typical of a state.

217. A.

The maximum loss for a long call spread is the difference in premiums (debit).

218. D.

The authorized stock of the corporation is the total amount allowed to be issue as defined in its corporate charter.

219. D.

Treasury STRIPS are the coupons stripped from Treasury receipts (known as either Treasury Income Growth Receipts - TIGRS, Certificates of Accrual on Treasury Securities - CATS or Lehman Investment Opportunity Notes - LIONs). In this case, the customer is purchasing a stream of revenue.

220. B.

The custodian's primary responsibility is safeguarding the physical assets of the fund.

221. D.

Investment tax credits (prior to their elimination via the Tax Reform Act of 1986) never applied to raw land but instead personal property.

222. D.

The value of the periodic payments made to the annuitant upon annuitization will fluctuate, depending on the performance of the securities that make up the accumulation units. The principal value of the variable annuity is relinquished by the contract holder upon annuitization.

223. A.

The formula is: NAV + SC equals the POP. 6% × $15 = $0.90 sales charge per share; $15 minus $0.90 per share = $14.10; $14.10 × 1,000 shares = $14,100; $14,100 × 1% (redemption fee) = $141; $14,100 - $141 = $13,959.

224. B.

Determine the number of shares into which the bond are convertible by dividing the par value ($1,000) by the conversion price ($25) = 40 shares. To determine the parity price, divide the call price of $1,050 by 40 shares = $26.25. Since the stock is trading above the parity price ($28 versus $26.25), the bondholders should convert their bonds to common stock resulting in a forced conversion.

225. D.

All of the choices listed are correct.

226. D.

In a transaction that is a seller's option, the seller can only deliver on the specified date unless the buyer is receives one business day's notice.

227. D.

The SIPC trustee will first notify the firm's customers, verify the records, distribute customer property, and finally handle all customers' SIPC claims.

228. D.

The stock was purchased and sold inside a year, representing a short-term capital gain of $1,000. Short-term capital gains are taxed at an individual's ordinary income tax rate, so in this example $1,000 × 25% = $250.

229. B.

MSRB Rule G-20, entitled Gifts, Gratuities, and Non-Cash Compensation limit gifts to $100 per person (other than an employee or partner) per year.

230. D.

The firms and their registered representatives are all guilty of violating the free-riding and withholding rules.

231. A.

CMOs issued with different tranches, varying maturities, and sequential retirement are known as vanilla CMOs.

232. B.

A spread transaction occurs when a customer buys and sells a put or a call simultaneously on the same underlying security. Either expiration dates or strike prices differ.

233. A.

Stock certificates that are held in street name are registered under the name of the broker/dealer.

234. B.

Annual interest payment divided by current market price = current yield. $100 ÷ $1,050 = 9.52%.

235. B.

The formula for determining the sales charge for an open-end investment company is (POP minus NAV)/(POP); $15.50 - $14.35 = $1.15 ÷ $15.50 = 7.42%.

236. C.

The role of a general partner is to act as agent of the partnership and manage assets of the partnership.

237. C.

The assets of a variable annuity are held in a separate account, which is segregated from the insurer's general account, which underlies the assets for its fixed insurance portfolio products including fixed annuities.

238. D.

The investor must be informed that the concentrated of investments in a particular fund family will result in the availability of sales charges breakpoints.

239. C.

Determine how many shares of common stock the preferred is convertible into by dividing the par price of the preferred stock ($100) by the conversion price ($50). Take that number (2) and divide it into the market price of the preferred stock ($102) and the parity price per share is $51.

240. A.

A broker/dealer may extend credit on a new issue if they have been participated in the distribution of the new issue for a period of 30 days.

241. D.

SIPC is not an U.S. government agency.

242. C.

A market that is "consolidating" is one that is neutral, neither moving up, nor down.

243. B.

To calculate the parity price of the common stock, take the current market price of the convertible bond divided by the conversion ratio. $800 ÷ 20 = $40.

244. B.

There are two orders, a simple limit order for 1,000 shares of XYZ at $38 and a buy stop order that was entered to purchase 1,000 shares of XYZ at 42 stop. The limit order is placed below the market price and executed when that price is reached. A limit buy is only executed at the requested price and is a bearish position, meaning that the customer believes that market prices are falling. This will be entered on the ticket as a "Good-Till-Canceled" or GTC order. The Buy-Stop order is a bullish market position with the customer believing that the market price is rising. Placing the "stop" elects the order when the price is reached ($42) and executed at the next tick, making it a market order. What the customer has done here is hedge his bet on the stock by betting on both sides of the market. Since the order was partially filled, each open ticket is reduced 700 shares. The remaining orders on the book for this customer with the broker/dealer is a 300 share GTC Buy Limit @ $38 and a 300 share Buy-Stop @ $42.

245. A.

A quote is given that contains no qualification is a firm quote.

246. D.

Legal opinions issued by bond counsel as to the ability of the issuer to borrow funds and the legality of the issue is considered an unqualified legal opinion.

247. D.

The Visible Supply is a 30 day outlook of new bond issues.

248. B.

The put writer, if exercised against, buys the stock at the strike p.rice ($30 per share). If the price goes to 0, the loss would be $3,000 minus the $300 received as a premium for a maximum loss of $2,700.

249. C.

Because it is a cumulative preferred stock issue, all prior year dividends must be paid first before a dividend can be paid to common stockholders. The company paid dividends of $5, $6 and $7 in successive years. Since the preferred stock has a par value of $100, 7% equals a $7 per share dividend, requiring $3 in past dividends to be paid plus $7 for a total of $10 paid last year.

250. A.

The Federal Farm Credit Consolidated System-Wide Bonds are only taxable at the federal level.

CPSIA information can be obtained at www.ICGtesting.com
Printed in the USA
LVOW09s0241191016

509376LV00014B/202/P